How to Find the
RIGHT
DIVORCE
LAWYER

Robin Page West, J.D.

CB
CONTEMPORARY BOOKS

346.0166
w

Library of Congress Cataloging-in-Publication Data

West, Robin Page.
   How to find the right divorce lawyer / Robin Page West.
      p.   cm.
   Includes index.
   ISBN 0-8092-3056-9
      1. Divorce suits—United States—Popular works.   2. Attorney and client—
United States—Popular works.   3. Lawyers—United States—Popular works.
I. Title.
   KF535.Z9W43   1997
   346.7301'66—dc20   96-44114
   [347.306166]   CIP

The anecdotes in this book, although inspired by actual events, are fictional examples created by the author to illustrate various points. Any similarity to any person or persons, alive or dead, is purely coincidental.

   The general legal principles cited in this book may not necessarily apply in your state or your particular situation. This book is not, and should not be used as, a substitute for legal advice. Should you be in need of legal advice, seek counsel from an attorney licensed in your state.

Material from *Children Held Hostage*, by Stanley Clawar and Brynne Rivlin, reprinted by permission of the American Bar Association. Copyright © 1991, American Bar Association. All rights reserved.

Cover design by Scott Rattray
Interior design by Mary Lockwood
Back cover photo © José Villarubia

This book is dedicated to my children, who gave me the strength and inspiration to keep fighting until the result was right.

Contents

Acknowledgments

I want to thank my office administrator, Dorothy Reed, for helping me, every day for years, keep my personal and professional life going smoothly during the onslaught of unpleasantries associated with my divorce and custody battle. I want to thank my parents, Bill and Marilyn West, for being there for me whenever and wherever I needed to be picked up and sent back out into battle. I want to thank my son's guidance counselor, Naomi Kochen, for encouraging me and making it possible for me to maintain a relationship with my son at school during those hellish years when the judicial system all but shut me out of his life. I also want to thank those mothers—you know who you are—who sought me out and opened my eyes to the fact that my children and I were by no means the only ones being brutalized by an unkind family-law system. I want to thank my friends, and the parents of my children's friends, who urged me to persevere in the litigation when I considered giving up. And finally, I would like to thank my current attorneys, Paul Mark Sandler, Raymond Daniel Burke, Lloyd J. Snow, and Lynn Weinberg, for being that needle in a haystack I thought I would never find.

Introduction

I write this book not only as a lawyer but also as a victim of the family-law judicial system. Just months after the birth of my daughter, I took her and my young son and fled—with just the clothes on our backs—what I felt was an abusive marriage. Even though my former husband was later found guilty of assaulting and battering me in the parking lot outside our son's kindergarten enrichment program and was required to participate in a spouse abuse program and psychological counseling as conditions of his probation, he nonetheless came out of the marriage with our paid-off house, more than half the money I had placed in a pension over the course of my legal career, and custody of our son. Although the judicial official who presided over our custody trial for three and one-half days recommended that custody of both children be awarded to me, a judge who did not hear a word of testimony or lay eyes on a single witness reversed that official and issued an order splitting the two children between their parents and providing for them to see each other only two weekends a month. The result of the judge's order would have been for my six-year-old son to grow up in the custody of a man found guilty of assaulting and battering his mother (me) in his presence. The judge's order also provided that our daughter would live with me, only to see her father and brother two weekends a month. Not only were their parents splitting up, but these children would also have to suffer even more at the hands of a judicial system that separated them from each other.

Have you read about similar stories or seen them on TV? Unfortunately, they are not exceptions but rather are all too common. How can the system bring about such outrageous results? As a lawyer who was personally dragged through the process, I believe that these things happen in part because the system contains no safeguards to ensure that a lawyer's work does any good for his or her client. Your lawyer may work hours on your case, but is he or she actually advancing your cause or simply defending against attacks by the other side and getting extensions of time to avoid having to focus on trying to win for you? In order to win, your lawyer must take control of the case and dictate the agenda. Unfortunately, your legal expenses will be just as high if your spouse's lawyer takes control and your lawyer simply reacts. And if both spouses' lawyers fail to take control, the case will develop a life of its own, resulting in enormous fees being paid by both spouses to lawyers who do nothing but mechanically follow procedures and never take stock of their clients' goals and objectives.

Does this sound overly grim? Are you comforting yourself with the belief that lawyers must do a good job because they passed the bar exam? That my children and I must have somehow deserved what we got? That the judge in our case must have had a good reason to split up the children? As hard as it is to believe, my case is just one of many that has ended in a bizarre result. How can this be?

A trial of any kind—divorce or otherwise—is not about the truth. It's about the two stories the opposing lawyers tell and how well they tell them. But it's also about the values and beliefs of the judge who hears a particular case. The judge who took my son away from me had previously testified before Congress against a bill that would presume spouse abusers unfit custodial parents. In opposing the bill (which passed in spite of his efforts), he said, "This resolution . . . could result in a spouse being denied his or her God-given right as a parent because of a push or a shove or a scratch or a bruise occurring in one moment of anger or frustration." Taking this one step further in my case, incredibly, he gave custody of the child to the parent found guilty of assault and deprived the nonabusive parent of her right to raise her son. Without even laying eyes on us or hearing any testimony, this judge also deprived two young children of their God-given right to grow up together as siblings. One can only speculate about his true motives. Perhaps he had no motives but simply issued his order in a rush, without the benefit of reflection. If he is biased, why is he allowed to sit in judgment in cases involving allegations of domestic violence? If he is not biased, why did he issue an order tearing my family apart and rewarding (or, at best, ignoring) what my ex-spouse did to me? If the judge's decision was the result of his not having enough time to think through the case, why didn't he defer to the judicial officer, who had spent three and one-half days hearing testimony and judging the credibility of witnesses? Perhaps you have heard other survivors of divorce make similar observations about the judges in their cases—and ask similar questions.

No matter which side of the issue you are on, no matter what your gender, race, sexual preference, or religion, once you become embroiled in a divorce or custody battle, you are entering a minefield of lawyers and judges who could not care less that your life and your children's lives have been turned upside down. Just as lawyers are expected to do, your spouse's lawyer will drag you through the mud, invade your privacy, and threaten to take your home, your children, your car, your clothes, your retirement money, and your savings. If you turn to a therapist for help, your therapy records may be subpoenaed and placed in the courthouse file for public consumption. The therapist may turn against you in court or be manipulated by your spouse's lawyer into saying things that hurt your case.

You and your children will be under attack and will need a good lawyer for protection. But even with a good lawyer, there is no guarantee of fair proceedings or a just result. Drawing on my horrifying observations of domestic-relations law and the lawyers and judges who function in that milieu, I have written this book to open your eyes and to help you protect yourself and your children. If you understand how the system works, why it is important to find a good lawyer, and what makes a lawyer good, then your chances of obtaining a just and fair result will be greatly improved.

You might be wondering how my story ended. I found a new lawyer (my fourth) and appealed the decision that took my son away from me. Unfortunately, although I won my appeal and the right to a new trial, the case was sent back to the same judge who had originally split up my children. Still not satisfied, I fired the lawyer who had won the appeal and went in search of even more forceful representation. This time I found the law firm I wish I had hired in the beginning. With the help of the lawyers there, who excelled in many of the areas at which I believe my other lawyers were ineffective, I negotiated a settlement agreement with my ex-husband that made our children's interests paramount, that preserved their right to have a relationship with each other and with both of their parents, and that does not invite conflict between their father and me.

Because it was a settlement agreement, as opposed to a trial or a hearing, that determined the outcome, both of us are presumably pleased with the result and neither will appeal. As a result, unless our circumstances change, our courtroom battle is at an end. We can both get on with the business of raising our children and living our separate lives.

1

Why You Need a Lawyer

Perhaps you believe that you don't need a divorce lawyer because you and your spouse are only having minor marital problems and are nowhere near the point of no return. Or perhaps you think a lawyer is an expensive and unnecessary luxury because you and your spouse agree about getting a divorce. Or maybe you think a lawyer would be a waste of money because you have no children. Or because you are willing to give up whatever is necessary just to get divorced. Or your spouse signed a prenuptial agreement giving everything to you. Even under these circumstances, it would nevertheless be prudent to have an attorney.

If you feel as though your marriage could be on the rocks, don't wait for certain disaster before finding a lawyer. I was so intent upon saving my marriage that I failed to even consider the possibility that I would need a divorce lawyer until things got so bad that I had to leave home. With two small children and nowhere to live, I didn't have the luxury of interviewing lawyer candidates in a careful and methodical way. I was in the middle of a crisis. Because I had not planned for an eventuality I considered too dreadful to contemplate, I paid the price. Had I consulted lawyers before I actually needed one, I believe my divorce would have been much less stressful. Had I been represented by competent and caring counsel from the beginning, I would have had only one problem to deal with—my ex. As it was, I had to deal not only with him but also with the problem of finding a decent lawyer.

Another benefit of finding your divorce lawyer before you're even sure you want a divorce is that you can obtain pre-separation advice. Your lawyer can show you ways to protect yourself financially and protect your children from as much disruption as possible. For example, had I known about the domestic violence laws in my state, rather than fleeing with my children, I might have been able to exclude my then-husband from the house. A lawyer can suggest ways to organize your finances so that, should a separation occur, your spouse will not be able to gain economic control over you by "cleaning you out." Once you and your spouse are on the verge of a divorce, it is often too late to take precautionary financial measures.

Even if you both agree to be divorced, and even if you have no children, you and your spouse will have to divide up your assets and bills. If either of you has a retirement fund, the other may be entitled to part of it. If you have joint credit, you may be responsible for each other's debts. If you have a house, you will have to decide who will stay and how the mortgage payments will be made. If you sell the house, who will pay the capital-gains taxes and how will the proceeds be divided? One of you may be entitled to alimony or support from the other, which could be a significant sum of money over a long period of time. Even if you and your spouse have a prenuptial agreement, what it means may be open to debate and it may not be legally binding. You need an attorney to recognize these and other issues and explain them to you.

Even if you and your spouse foresee all the possible issues and agree on all the answers, you will need a legally enforceable settlement agreement to make sure neither person changes his or her mind later and comes back asking for more. Moreover, some things to which you are willing to agree may not be legal. For example, if your spouse says, "Give me custody of both kids and I will never ask you for child support," you could be making a mistake if you agree. In many jurisdictions, a parent cannot legally waive child support. You could very well wind up losing custody *and* paying child support, all because you did not know your legal rights.

Even if you and your spouse manage to reach an agreement without resorting to the courts, you will need lawyers to reduce the agreement to a legally enforceable document. If your settlement is not in the proper legal form or is otherwise invalid because of a technicality, you or your spouse might be able to come back later and raise all these issues anew. This is one situation in which an ounce of prevention is definitely worth a pound of cure. Get your agreement in writing, and have your lawyer review it to make sure it will stick.

Once the wheels of divorce litigation start to turn, you jeopardize your living arrangements, your finances, and your status as a parent. The court has the power to take everything away from you and give it to your spouse. The job of your spouse's lawyer is to find reasons for the judge to take these things from you.

Suppose you are well educated, you don't drink or use drugs, and your life consists of going to work to support your family and then coming home to take care of your children. You don't carouse or go to the track. You are truly a family person with family values. Then one day you learn that your spouse is having an ongoing affair and you file for divorce and custody. You never even consider the possibility that you could lose custody of your children.

Think again. Ms. A., a political lobbyist, lost custody of her daughter in just such a situation when a judge found that her career had more of a deleterious effect on the marriage than the husband's adultery. The little girl lived with the adulterer until she was old enough to hire a lawyer of her own and petition for a change of custody.

Although men have for a long time faced an uphill battle when it came to getting custody (or even joint custody), now women face the same, perhaps even more difficult, hurdles. Legal commentators speculate that the more successful a woman is in her profession, the more that fact will be used to demonstrate her unfitness as a parent. Senator Orrin Hatch's chief of staff, Sharon Prost, lost custody of her sons after just such an argument was made against her.* O. J. Simpson prosecutor Marcia Clark was the target of a similar attack when her husband claimed that her job interfered with her ability to raise their two sons.**

Even mothers who are not high-profile professionals have lost their children for sins even less egregious than going to work to support them. College student Jennifer Ireland lost custody of her daughter because she put the four-year-old in day care while she attended classes at a local university. When Ms. Ireland sought to collect child support

*Prost v. Greene, No. DR-2957-92d (Washington, D.C., Superior Court, July 6, 1994)

**In re Marriage of Clark, No. BD165849 (California, Los Angeles County Superior Court, filed June 9, 1994)

from the girl's father (to whom she was never married), he responded with a custody suit. Even though the girl's father did not stay home to take care of the child either, it was the mother the judge saw fit to punish, not the father.* In another case, a Florida judge awarded custody of an eleven-year-old girl to her father, who had been convicted of murdering his ex-wife during a custody dispute over another daughter, rather than allow the eleven-year-old to live with her lesbian mother. Apparently finding lesbianism more heinous than murder, the trial judge did not mention the father's murder conviction in the custody decision, which said that the child "should be given the opportunity and the option to live in a nonlesbian world."** The mother died soon thereafter of a heart attack.

There are two sides to every divorce and custody dispute. Whether you are male or female, gay or straight, working outside or inside the home, you could be victimized by a judge whose values are nothing like your own. The sad reality of the court system is that no parent has control over what judge he or she will get, what that judge's biases are, or what that judge will ultimately decide. The more assertive and tenacious your lawyer is, though, the more likely he or she will be to have an impact on the judge's decision and the better able he or she will be to "protect the record" to set the stage for an appeal.

Dismantling a family is infinitely more complicated, expensive, and emotionally wrenching than getting married. Obtaining a divorce decree or custody order bears no resemblance to the simple process of obtaining a marriage license. And, unfortunately, these legal twists and turns come at a time in your life when you are emotionally ill-equipped to handle the challenge. When you turn to a lawyer for help,

Ireland v. Smith, 451 Mich. 457, 574 N.W. 2d 686 (1996)
**Ward v. Ward*, No. 95-04184 Florida District Court App., Jan. 24, 1996

your spouse may become defensive and retaliate, making matters ugly even if you didn't want them to be. The legal system often leads spouses (or their lawyers) to make accusations and counter-accusations, demands and counter-demands. As life as you once knew it is falling apart around you and the person you once loved the most turns into your fiercest enemy, you may very well wonder whether your own judgment is faulty.

In the middle of dealing with all the personal and emotional issues involved in separating from your spouse, you may find yourself confronted with the unpleasant notion that, on top of it all, your lawyer isn't even doing a good job. You might feel that your supposed advocate isn't there when you need advice, gives in too easily, or doesn't make things move quickly enough. Are your expectations unrealistic? Are you under too much stress to see things objectively, or is the lawyer you hired in fact simply taking your money and going through the motions?

Among other things, this book will explain what to look for in a lawyer (Chapter 4), how to tell if your lawyer is doing a proper job (Chapter 8), how to switch lawyers if you need to (Chapter 9), and what recourse you have if a lawyer has botched something irretrievably (Chapter 9).

Too many marriages end in divorce. The courts are clogged with divorce cases and do not (perhaps cannot) deal with family-law problems in a humane and efficient way. While politicians argue about how to improve the system, divorcing spouses and their children are stuck with it the way it is. No one ever *wants* to have to hire a divorce lawyer, but you owe it to yourself and your children to hire the best one you can find and afford.

2

How to End the Conflict

Making decisions in divorce and custody litigation is a classic chicken-and-egg problem. You can't tell your lawyer what you want if you don't know what your rights are, and you can't know what your rights are until a lawyer explains them to you. But you can't hire a lawyer until you understand how the system works, so that you can figure out who would be a good lawyer to advocate your interests in the system. So where do you start?

Understanding the System

This chapter contains an overview of the legal system as it pertains to divorce and child custody. If you read it now, you will acquire some perspective on what the lawyer you are going to hire will be doing during the course of your representation. And understanding how the system works will help you choose a lawyer more intelligently. If, however, you are too overwhelmed right now to try to learn about the system, you can skip directly to Chapter 3, where the information on how to select the right lawyer begins. You can go ahead and hire a lawyer and then let him or her teach you about how the system works on a need-to-know basis. Bear in mind, though, that the more you understand ahead of time about the family-law system, the better your judgment will be when it comes to selecting an attorney.

Even though the romance and love between you and your spouse have disappeared and you may no longer be living together, until you are legally divorced, you are still married. The legal ramifications of being married vary from state to state, but generally speaking, until you are divorced you and your spouse have certain rights to each other's money, deferred compensation, pensions, insurance benefits, real estate, and other property. In general, until you are divorced not only can you not remarry but also anything you obtain may be subject to a claim of ownership, in whole or in part, by your spouse, and the future ownership of assets and property already obtained may be unclear. Even if you have a prenuptial agreement, your spouse may succeed in having it declared invalid. In short, the potential to lose things you think are yours remains until the divorce is final and all appeals have been exhausted.

The law specifying what you or your spouse must prove to be entitled to a divorce varies from state to state. Some states require proof of certain "grounds," such as adultery; other states have "no-fault" divorces. Some states require the two parties to live separately (and under specific conditions) for a certain period of time. Before filing for divorce in some states, you must first have lived there for a certain amount of time. Sometimes, such as when the parties involved have moved recently, it is unclear which state's law applies.

You will need a lawyer to tell you what the law in your state is and how it applies to the facts of your marriage. That is the only way you can determine whether you or your spouse will be likely to succeed in getting a divorce, support, and/or custody.

Contested vs. Uncontested Divorce

There are two kinds of divorces—contested and uncontested. A *contested* divorce is one in which the parties cannot agree, either about getting divorced or about the terms of the divorce, such as the division of assets or the custody of children. In an *uncontested* divorce, the spouses agree on everything and do not need the court to divide assets or make determinations about spousal or child support or custody. In general, an uncontested divorce will proceed through the system more quickly and cost less in attorneys' fees than a contested divorce.

Often couples will begin the process of a contested divorce and then, before the actual trial, reach agreement on the terms—financial and otherwise—of the divorce. This is called a *settlement*. One of the biggest advantages of a settlement is that neither spouse will appeal it, because both by definition agree to it and thus are presumably happy with it. Both parties can therefore be assured of finality and an end to litigation. If you reach a settlement with your spouse, it is essential to have the agreement memorialized in such a way that it makes the settlement legally binding and enforceable.

Trial Preparation and Discovery

In a contested case, after one spouse files for divorce, the often acrimonious, torturous, and expensive process of *dis-*

covery begins. Each side sends the other lengthy lists of questions called *interrogatories*, which have been drafted at huge expense by the lawyers and which must be answered under oath. A typical set of interrogatories is reproduced in Appendix F. Interrogatories are composed of questions about finances, assets, pensions, and similar issues. Through their lawyers, the spouses can also ask each other to produce documents such as bank statements, credit-card bills, receipts, tax returns, paycheck stubs, and the like. The lawyers will (again at huge expense) sift through the interrogatory answers and documents and then question the spouses in person under oath at something called a *deposition*. Other people who have relevant information, such as neighbors, accountants, or other witnesses, may also be questioned at a deposition. A deposition takes place in the presence of a stenographer (a court reporter), who later transcribes what was said into a typewritten booklet. The charge for transcribing a several-hours-long deposition is in the hundreds of dollars. In some cases, depositions last for days, during which the lawyers are being paid by the hour.

Usually the lawyers are looking for hidden or "wasted" assets, in order to determine how much money, earning power, and other assets each spouse has (or had) so that they can be divvied up. In contested custody cases, the lawyers will be looking for evidence that the parent on the other side is not fit to have custody.

Trial preparation efforts are important because the information that comes out at a trial depends very much on how well the lawyers understand and present the facts—both favorable and unfavorable—to the judge. Even the best case can be lost if the lawyer is unprepared, careless, incompetent, or otherwise ineffectual. Moreover, the best-prepared lawyer with the best case can also lose if the other lawyer is more effective or the judge is biased.

Regardless of whether you ultimately settle your case or litigate it to the bitter end, trial preparation is essential. Lawyers who do not prepare for court hearings or trial (because they are lazy, trying to save a client money, or just hoping a case will settle without a trial) turn their clients into sitting ducks. If the other side senses that you or your attorney wishes to avoid a trial, cannot afford one, or is not preparing for one, you will be at a distinct legal disadvantage. In addition to being ill-equipped for a possible trial, the unprepared lawyer cannot negotiate a settlement from a position of strength. If you come to the peace talks with no bombs or bullets, will anyone listen to what you have to say? A lawyer who is unprepared for a hearing or trial is inviting the opposition to take advantage of his or her client.

In spite of this, it is not unusual for divorce lawyers to spend their days flitting from one court proceeding to another, handling hearings on many different cases in the same day, having spent no time at all in preparation. I have seen lawyers go into court to argue over custody without knowing the names or ages of the children involved. I have heard lawyers make up "facts" because they hadn't bothered to learn the real facts. I have watched lawyers stand mute in court, while the other side filled the air with lies, because they were so poorly prepared that they did not even know they were hearing lies.

Because trial preparation is time-consuming and expensive, you or your attorney may be tempted to cut corners. Such a move could be penny-wise and pound-foolish, however, because if your case is well prepared, you should be able to proceed from a position of strength to fashion a satisfactory settlement instead of going to trial.

Expert Witnesses

Part of preparing for trial is locating expert witnesses. An expert witness is someone who is allowed to express a professional opinion at the trial. In divorce and custody cases, expert witnesses include psychologists, economists, accountants, social workers, and pediatricians, among others. In custody cases, the court will often allow testimony by psychologists or social workers to help determine what decisions are in the best interests of the children. Experts such as psychologists usually charge $150 to $300 per hour to evaluate the people involved and formulate an opinion regarding who should have custody. A custody evaluation by a psychologist ordinarily costs thousands of dollars.

Do not assume that just because someone has a Ph.D. he or she will necessarily view your family situation the same way you do. Just as there are two sides to every story, there are also several ways to look at any given family dynamic. And just as judges have biases, so do expert witnesses. Do not assume that such a person is impartial or has no financial incentive or other reason to give an opinion in favor of your spouse and against you. It is probably safe to assume that if your spouse is paying for an expert, that expert will find a reason why you should not have custody. Otherwise, why would your spouse be paying this person? Even if you and your spouse are splitting the cost of an expert or an expert was appointed by the court, do not assume that the expert will be impartial. Talk to your lawyer about hiring an expert of your own. (See Chapter 7 for more on the role of the paid expert.)

Perhaps you have nothing going in your favor in a custody case. Let's say you are unemployed and your spouse, who works, takes the children to work and watches them there while you veg out at home every day. You want custody, though, so you won't have to pay child support. If you get custody, you plan to let your mother watch the kids and use the child-support money to make the rent and car payments. How can you get custody? Your best tactic may be to hire an expert to trash your spouse for being a compulsive workaholic. Sound far-fetched? It shouldn't.

If your spouse hires an expert, beware. Take it seriously, and do whatever it takes to get your own expert to counteract your spouse's. Even better, be the one to get an expert first. If your lawyer doesn't know enough to get an expert or doesn't know how to find a good one, watch out: your lawyer is involved in a high-stakes game without a firm grasp of how it's played.

Hearings and Trial

Once the discovery process is complete, each lawyer will use legal precedent to construct an argument about what his or her client is entitled to. Then a trial will take place, during which the lawyers will present the judge, master, or other person hearing the case with information favorable to their argument. This information is presented in the form of witness testimony focusing on whatever the lawyers decide to focus on. This is called *putting on a case*.

The trial may not take place for a year or more after a divorce case is filed in court. Before the trial, numerous shorter court proceedings, called *hearings*, may take place. The purpose of these hearings is to resolve emergency issues such as where the children will live pending the results of the trial. Hearings will also be held to address legal issues that arise during the course of trial preparation. For example, suppose your lawyer has sent the other side thirty questions to answer under oath, but the questions have been ignored because the other side claims that the questions are improper. If your attorney requests it, the court may hold a hearing to determine whether the other side should be compelled to answer the questions.

The trial itself will proceed in front of a judge, master, magistrate, or other hearing officer and will begin with each lawyer making an *opening statement* regarding what he or she intends to prove. Usually the lawyer for the person who filed suit makes the first opening statement. Be prepared for the opening statement by your spouse's lawyer to include disparaging, insulting, and untrue statements about your honesty, moral character, earning capacity, income, assets, and fitness as a parent.

After the opening statements, each side will present his or her case, with the party who initiated the lawsuit (the plaintiff) going first. Each lawyer will call witnesses to the stand and ask them questions. This is called *direct examination*. The lawyer presenting a witness is not permitted to ask leading questions such as, "On December tenth, did your wife threaten you with a gun?" Rather, the lawyer must ask, "What, if anything unusual, happened on December tenth?"

Because your own lawyer is not allowed to ask you leading questions while you are on the witness stand, you may find it difficult to figure out how to answer. If your lawyer asks, "What, if anything, occurred?" or something similarly vague, you may not know what he or she is driving at and get flustered. This is why it is valuable to meet with your lawyer before the trial and go over your testimony. If you believe you will need notes to help you remember dates or other information, discuss this with your attorney.

Once the attorney presenting a particular witness has finished direct examination, the other attorney is permitted to cross-examine that witness. In contrast to direct examination, *cross-examination* may include leading questions such as, "Isn't it a fact that, as a teenager, you used cocaine?" The other side's lawyer may ask you a number of questions like this—questions that have absolutely no basis in fact—just to make the judge think that you might have done such things. If this happens, your lawyer should put a stop to it by objecting. But even if your lawyer does not object, try to stay cool and calm. You will make a better impression on the judge if you do not lose your temper or become abusive.

Your lawyer may be permitted to ask additional questions of you or another witness who has just been cross-examined. This is called *redirect*. The other lawyer may then cross-examine that witness on the subject of the redirect testimony; this is called *recross*. Once the plaintiff finishes presenting his or her witnesses and the cross-examination, redirect, and recross have been completed for each witness, then the other side presents its case and the initiating side gets to cross-examine those witnesses. Redirect and recross may once again follow.

Sometimes witnesses are taken out of sequence to allow for scheduling problems. This is especially likely to happen if doctors are involved and may sometimes be unavoidable, but a lawyer should not allow his or her presentation of evidence to be continually interrupted by witnesses taken out of turn by the other side. Your lawyer should focus on telling your side of the story in a logical and compelling way through the use of witnesses chosen because of what they know and how well they can communicate this information to the judge. As with any story, your case will not be as powerful or convincing if it is plagued by repeated interruptions.

Once each side has presented its case, the side that went first may present more testimony to rebut any new issues that were raised by the side that went second. This is called *rebut-tal*. Then the opposing party may also present additional testimony to rebut any new issues raised during rebuttal; this is called *surrebuttal*. And each side may, of course, cross-examine the other's witnesses.

Once this process is complete, the lawyers make their *closing arguments*, which usually consist of blistering and unfair personal attacks on the opposing party. Do not be surprised if the lawyers mischaracterize, misstate, or lie about what various witnesses have said on the stand. Many lawyers believe that, if they can get away with it, they have a duty to their clients to try these tactics. It is hard to say whether it is worse to be represented by a lawyer who aggressively twists the truth or to not have such a lawyer on your side. In any event, during closing arguments, you must sit mute while the other lawyer drones on with unfair innuendo and lies about you. This is certain to be one of the most painful and humiliating experiences you will ever endure. Then it's up to your lawyer to go back and correct any misimpressions the other lawyer left with the judge. Will your attorney be up to the task?

Appeal

After the trial, if you, your spouse, or both of you are not happy with the result, either or both of you may appeal. The purpose of an *appeal* is to determine whether the trial judge made a legal error such as misinterpreting the law or allowing into evidence testimony that should not have been admitted. If the appellate court determines that the trial judge did make a material legal error (that is, one that affected the outcome of the trial), it may send the case back to the same judge (or some other judge in the original judge's court) with instructions to correct the mistake. The way to correct the mistake is often for the judge to schedule the case for a whole new trial.

An appeal is generally not a vehicle for questioning the trial judge's factual conclusions. Suppose a trial judge concludes that a father is the better of two parents and awards him custody. In order to prevail on appeal, the mother must do more than simply argue to the appellate court that she is in fact the better parent; she must demonstrate that the trial judge reached the wrong conclusion because he or she made a mistake in applying the law during the trial.

Let's say that the judge in this hypothetical case found that the father was a better parent based on the testimony of six of the father's friends. Suppose the mother also had six friends she wanted to testify at the trial on her behalf, but the judge would not allow their testimony. Her lawyer objected and told the judge what these witnesses would say if they were allowed to testify, but the judge still would not allow them to testify. On appeal, the mother would argue that the judge erred by not letting her friends testify.

It is very important that her lawyer told the trial judge what these witnesses would say and objected at the trial to the judge's refusal to let them testify. If the lawyer hadn't objected, thus giving the judge an opportunity to correct the mistake, the mother would not be able to raise the issue later in the appellate court. Fortunately, the mother's attorney in this example "preserved the record" by objecting and offering the substance of the testimony to the court, thus paving the way for a successful appeal.

It is likely that the appellate court would agree that the trial judge should have listened to the mother's witnesses as well as the father's and would therefore issue an order *vacat-*

ing (or throwing out) the custody award to the father. In addition, the court would *remand*, or send back, the case to the trial judge, with instructions to let the mother's friends testify. Having won her appeal, now the mother must go through a whole new trial, possibly in front of the same judge. The fact that she won her appeal does not mean that she will win custody; it means only that she gets to have a new trial.

The appellate court will generally not second-guess factual conclusions that the trial judge has reached, because the appellate court does not take testimony or hear witnesses. Rather, the appellate court reads and listens to the arguments of the lawyers to determine if the trial judge made a legal error that affected the outcome of the trial. If so, in most cases the case will be returned to the trial court to have the error corrected.

The appellate process takes approximately one to two years. In contested custody cases, once a case has gone all the way through the appeal process and is sent back for a new trial, the circumstances of the case—such as the ages of the children or the financial situations of the parents—may have changed significantly. In such cases, having the case remanded can take as much time and cost as much money as starting from scratch.

After any trial, the losing spouse may use the threat of an appeal as a negotiating tactic to induce the winning spouse to give up all or part of what has been won. For example, let's say a judge splits up a couple's assets and gives fifty thousand dollars of the husband's pension to the wife. The husband can then threaten to appeal unless the wife settles the case by agreeing that he has to give her only forty thousand dollars. Then the wife has to decide whether to pay lawyers to fight the appeal for the next year or simply give up part of the pension and thus put an end to the legal battle.

If the wife refuses to settle and the husband loses his appeal, the wife will still be out the legal expenses of fighting the appeal. Although she may succeed in having the court order the husband to pay her legal expenses, there is no guarantee that this will happen. Moreover, because there is a possibility that the husband might win the appeal, the wife may not be able to get her hands on *any* of the pension funds while the appeal is pending. Thus being able to get the funds immediately and not having to litigate an appeal may make it worthwhile for the wife to give up the ten thousand dollars.

As you can see from these examples, it is important that your attorney understand the appellate process. Your lawyer needs to know enough about appeals to be able to preserve your case for appeal and also to be able to use the threat of appeal to soften the blow of a loss. If you win your case, your lawyer will advise you how to handle the threat of an appeal. Should you give up part of your winnings and settle? Or is your spouse just bluffing? If you choose not to give in, how much would an appeal cost? What are the chances of losing? Your lawyer must have enough experience at the appellate level to be able to answer these questions to your satisfaction.

Mediation and Counseling

In some jurisdictions, before the trial preparation or discovery process can even begin, the law requires that both parties participate in counseling or attempt to resolve their differences with a trained mediator. Counselors and mediators are not always funded by the state and will therefore charge for their time, usually at rates commensurate with lawyers'.

The idea behind mediation and counseling is to have trained professionals help defuse the emotional tension between the two parties and find areas of agreement that the parties may not have realized existed. These methods sometimes work, but they can also be expensive and time-consuming. Your lawyer should be able to tell you the success rates of various mediators and counselors in your area. Whether or not to engage in counseling or mediation, or both, is a decision that deserves serious consideration. If these methods do not result in a settlement, all the hard work and expense of litigation still lie ahead. If your would-be ex insists on being in total control or is abusive, you might be better off bypassing these alternative forms of dispute resolution if you can.

Spouses bent on prolonging the agony of divorce can and do manipulate the system into a form of financial and emotional torture for their former partners. Savvy divorce lawyers know how to wear down the other side—emotionally, financially, and physically—by scheduling expensive mediation sessions that go nowhere. Should this happen to you, it is important that you have a lawyer who is perceptive enough to recognize and put a halt to such manipulation rather than advising you to participate in counseling or mediation sessions out of a misplaced spirit of cooperation and compromise.

Some states have rules exempting abuse victims from having to participate in mediation or counseling with their abusers. If you have been abused and believe that joint counseling or mediation would merely be an opportunity for your spouse to continue the abuse, make sure your lawyer checks the law to see if you can be excused from court-ordered counseling or mediation.

Similarly, issues you deal with in the context of couples counseling or individual therapy—in a setting you believe to be confidential—can come back to haunt you in divorce court when the other side calls your therapist as a witness or subpoenas your therapy records and then hires an expert to put a damaging spin on what those records mean.

Suppose your spouse threatens to commit suicide if you don't let your son live with him or her. You go into therapy to try to figure out what to do. You spend months going over the issues with your therapist, trying to reach the right conclusion, and your therapist compiles reams of notes on what was said during those sessions. Later, the opposing lawyer may subpoena your therapy records and provide them to your spouse's hired expert to be interpreted in a damaging way. For example, if your final decision is to give up your son, that act—even though done to prevent your spouse's suicide—can and will be used to demonstrate that you don't care about your son. On the other hand, if you refuse to let your son see that same suicidal spouse because you think your spouse is mentally unstable and could be dangerous to your son, your refusal can and will be used against you to demonstrate that you are trying to deprive your son of his right to a relationship with his other parent.

Throughout the divorce process, you will be facing damned-if-you-do-and-damned-if-you-don't choices. The more decisions you make without the direct input of your attorney, the more risks you are taking. Therefore, if you decide to go into therapy, counseling, or mediation without your attorney, make sure you first understand the potential repercussions of that decision.

Masters or Magistrates

In many jurisdictions, in addition to the trial and the alternative dispute mechanisms described above, there is another layer of the judicial system known as *masters* or *magistrates*. These people are "junior judges" whose job it is to hear the evidence and make "proposed findings," or recommendations, to a judge. In some cases, using masters or magistrates prolong matters, whereas in others it speeds things up. Discuss with your lawyer whether using a master or magistrate is an option in your case and, if so, whether you should choose to do so.

The idea behind the use of masters and magistrates is to save judges the time it takes to sift through all the evidence. Sometimes the system works well, because masters and magistrates have more time to think about what they are doing than judges do. Other times, however, masters and magistrates make ridiculous mistakes.

Since a master's or magistrate's decision is not final until a judge adopts it, going through a trial presided over by a master or magistrate can wind up being an expensive exercise that leads nowhere except to a new trial in front of a judge. It is important that you understand how the system works in your jurisdiction. Even if you win in front of the master or magistrate, don't be surprised to learn that that was only the first round.

Judicial Indifference

Omnipresent in the arena of divorce and custody is the notion that it takes two people to have an argument and that at any time one person can stop the conflict by giving the other person what he or she wants. Many times, judges allow themselves to be seduced by this simplistic concept. Rather than try to determine who is right and who is wrong, some judges (because of lack of interest or lack of time) will apply pressure to both parties—in the form of verbal abuse, threats of financial sanctions, or sentencing the couple to attend parenting classes at night—until one party buckles under the pressure and lets the other have his or her way.

Lawyers can do little to protect you from this judicial attitude short of keeping you out of the courtroom. And the only way to stay out of court is for your attorney to prepare so well for court that the other side would rather settle than have a showdown. Don't believe for one minute that all you have to do to get justice is tell your story to a judge. That's just not the way it works. (Chapter 7 goes into detail about why this is so.)

Settlement

Once the litigation has begun, most spouses begin to figure out that if they could reach agreement, they would save themselves a great deal of money and aggravation. They understand, on some level, that they should settle the case instead of fighting it out in court. On another level, however, they are unable to settle. Why? Emotions are too raw. They distrust each other. One or both want a day in court to prove that they are right. Feelings like these frequently prevent divorcing spouses from settling their cases before going to trial. And when they are able to settle the case, it is often just days, sometimes even moments, before the trial.

Why then and not before? The impending trial, which promises to be expensive and stressful and guarantees an uncertain result, creates an incentive for both parties to work out their problems. Both parties eventually realize that, with a settlement, they will be able to exercise some degree of control over the result. This is not so if a judge decides for them. With the trial a year away, it is difficult to get the parties and their lawyers focused enough to talk about settlement. As a result, it often takes the same amount of time for a contested divorce to be settled as it would have for that same case to get to trial. This is rarely less than one year and can be as long as several years if appeals are involved.

(That criminal defendants have the right to a speedy trial while law-abiding citizens and innocent children are sentenced routinely to an excruciatingly long divorce process that causes untold misery and costs families their life savings is one of the great injustices in the twentieth-century United States. But if the family-law system were meaningfully improved, it would put an end to the feeding frenzy of divorce lawyers and mental-health professionals working in this field. Perhaps this explains why relief is so slow in coming.)

Setting the Legal Tone

Now that you have a grasp of how the system works, you need to hire an attorney and set the tone for the litigation. It is essential that you and your attorney set the tone instead of allowing your spouse to do it.

If you are determined to have a civilized, nonadversarial divorce, you must set that tone at the beginning. If you don't, your spouse may misread you and set an adversarial tone. Once that happens, both of you could waste a lot of time and money getting back onto a nonadversarial footing. On the other hand, if your spouse has been bullying you for years and you have consistently given in, now may be the time to make the statement that you aren't giving in anymore. Have your lawyer set that tone from the outset. Remember: the more bullying you accept, the more you will be expected to accept. Let your spouse know, through your lawyer's actions, that you intend to be in control now.

How your lawyer will go about setting the tone will depend on the particular facts of your case. If you intend to be adversarial and in control, your lawyer may set this tone by filing and serving the divorce papers and a slew of discovery requests on your spouse to show that you mean business. On the other hand, if you want to try to work things out amicably, your lawyer may send a letter to your spouse's lawyer asking, "What do we need to do to end this unpleasant matter for these nice people?" If your spouse's attorney writes back in a combative tone, your lawyer will need to reevaluate whether the nice approach is going to work. Many times in divorce, nice guys do finish last. In short, a divorce can be handled in myriad different ways, and you need the right lawyer to size up the situation and act accordingly.

3

Finding the Right Lawyer for You

Gathering Information

Now that you have an overview of the system and under-stand the necessity of finding the right divorce lawyer for you and your case, how do you go about accomplishing this task? This chapter describes the information you will need and outlines how to get it. Chapter 4 shows you how to use that information to choose the right lawyer.

Collecting Names

To start your search for the right lawyer, gather the names of as many candidates as possible and then find out every-thing you can about each one. A lawyer might practice in more than one area of law, but this is not necessarily a problem as long as a substantial percentage of his or her caseload is in family or domestic law. What you need is a good *divorce* lawyer, not just a garden-variety good lawyer.

Family Members, Friends, and Acquaintances

Family members, friends, and acquaintances may be able to recommend lawyers, although you may be reluctant to divulge to anyone that you are even looking for a divorce lawyer out of fear that the information might get back to your spouse. This is a judgment call only you can make. Keep in mind, however, that you will need the support of family and friends if you go through a divorce, and now—before you really need it—might be the best time to start building that network of support. Once the wheels of divorce start to turn, friends and family are often forced to choose sides. If you wait too long to turn to others for help, you may find that some people who might have supported you have already pledged their loyalty to your spouse.

Do not hesitate to ask people you know only slightly to recommend lawyers as well. People who have been through a divorce are often happy to talk about it if they feel they can help someone else.

Because going through a divorce or custody battle (or both) can be extremely unpleasant, and human nature is such that we tend to block out painful memories, the family members, friends, and acquaintances you ask for referrals may not readily remember details. You may need to ask people very specific questions about their lawyers before any helpful information is forthcoming. Use the "Information from Family Members, Friends, and Acquaintances" form (Appendix A) as a guide for what to ask. Make multiple copies of the form, one for each lawyer candidate. Fill in the information for each lawyer as you receive it, but don't be concerned if you can't answer all the questions. Simply get as much information as you can. Then, before you interview each candidate, prepare your interview questions based on the information you already have.

Advertisements

Some lawyers advertise—in the newspaper, in the phone book, on television, or by direct mail. In general, lawyers who advertise have "volume" practices. This means they handle a large number of relatively uncomplicated cases. Large numbers of people respond to their ads; then they choose the cases that look the easiest (and most lucrative) to handle. If your situation is uncomplicated, you may get good service from someone who advertises. Although you are less likely to receive personalized, detail-oriented service from a lawyer who has a volume practice than you would from a lawyer managing fewer cases at one time, such a lawyer may (as a result of the volume) charge less. Put any such candidates who interest you on your list for further investigation, but do not let that be the end of your search.

Speakers and Columnists

Some lawyers write columns for newsletters or give speeches to community groups. If the subject of a speech or article is domestic law, consider the speaker or author very seriously as a candidate. The fact that an attorney writes or speaks on the topic of family law indicates a commitment to the field, an ability and willingness to do work, and a connection with people. Consider how much more time, expertise, and energy are involved in giving a speech or writing an article than in running an ad. You want a committed lawyer on your side.

Referral Services

Most states, and some counties and cities, have a lawyer referral service sponsored by the jurisdiction's bar association. To locate a referral service in your area, call your state's bar association. Phone numbers for state bar associations are listed in the "Other Resources" section at the back of this book. When you call your state's bar association and ask for information about referrals, you will probably be given more numbers to call, but eventually you should reach a referral service of some kind. (You may also find listings for referral services in the Yellow Pages under "Lawyers.") Lawyers who are listed with referral services usually have no special qualifications other than having paid a fee to be placed on the list. If you get a lawyer's name from a referral service, you still need to do your homework by interviewing him or her.

Therapists, Support Groups, and Doctors

If you are in a support group, the group leader and other group members may be able to give you recommendations. Medical doctors, social workers, or therapists may also be able to provide you with names of potential lawyers. These sources of referrals are routinely in contact with people going through painful divorces. They hear war stories and may even have testified themselves in court as experts in divorce cases. If you don't ask, they may not voluntarily foist their opinions on you; but if you do ask, they may be able to tell you which lawyers impressed them, which did not, and why.

Professional Directories

If you can locate a directory of attorneys in your area, it may prove very useful. The most widely recognized legal directory is the *Martindale-Hubbell Law Directory*, which is available in some public libraries and law-school libraries (sometimes on CD-ROM). *Martindale-Hubbell* lists lawyers by city, state, and field of expertise. The directory strives to include in its blue pages the name, address, and birth date of all attorneys, but lawyers must pay to have biographical information included in the directory's white pages. *Martindale-Hubbell* sends out the names of lawyers who purchase space in the white pages to other lawyers in the same geographic area with a request that they rate the lawyer. These ratings are published in the directory's blue pages. *AV* is the highest rating conferred by *Martindale-Hubbell*.

Not all lawyers make the effort to have themselves included in *Martindale-Hubbell*, but those who do are generally respected by their peers and have established practices. The *Martindale-Hubbell Bar Register of Preeminent Lawyers* is a separate publication that lists only those lawyers who received the highest rating in the *Martindale-Hubbell Law Directory*. (Lawyers must also pay a fee to be included in this publication.)

Bar Associations, Professional Trade Associations, and Law Schools

Another extremely useful source of attorney candidates is the roster of your state or local bar association's family, domestic, or matrimonial law section or committee. This roster may or may not be publicly available, depending on the particular bar association's policies. Attorneys who belong to such sections and committees devote unpaid time to working with other lawyers in their specialty putting on seminars, writing articles, advocating reforms, and other similar activities. In general, lawyers are active members of such sections or committees because they are genuinely interested in and committed to family or domestic-relations law. As a result, they will most likely have more experience in and commitment to this area of law than lawyers who simply place their names on a referral list.

It may take a few phone calls to determine whether a family, domestic, or matrimonial law section or committee exists in your locality and even more phone calls to get a copy of the list (if it is available to the public). If you can obtain such a list, you will have a pool of local lawyers who are knowledgeable about domestic-relations law to draw from. If the roster is not available to the public, you may nevertheless be able to find out the name of the section or committee chair (a good candidate), who may in turn be able to refer you to other members. In searching for lawyers who are active on such sections or committees, remember to check not only with your state bar association but also with your city or county bar association. A list of addresses and phone numbers for state bar associations appears in the "Other Resources" section at the back of this book. To locate a city or county bar association in your area, contact your state bar association.

Some bar associations and law-school legal clinics have programs that provide free or low-cost assistance in divorce and custody matters. To find out if any such programs exist in your area, call your state and local bar associations and any nearby law schools. In general, such programs are not as well equipped to handle complex divorces and contested custody cases as a seasoned attorney working at his or her normal hourly rate would be.

A handful of states—Arizona, California, Florida, Louisiana, New Jersey, New Mexico, North Carolina, South Carolina, and Texas—certify lawyers as specialists in family or domestic-relations law. (Other states may institute such certification in the future.) In general, to be certified as a specialist, an attorney must pass an exam and demonstrate that he or she has a certain amount of experience in family law. To find out if your state certifies family-law specialists, contact your state bar association or the attorney-licensing authority in your state.

The American Academy of Matrimonial Lawyers is an organization of family lawyers that requires members to devote a large percentage of their practice to domestic-relations law and to have done so for at least ten years. To become a member of the Academy, an attorney must pass an examination and submit references from other lawyers and judges. To find out if there is a chapter in your area, contact the Academy at (312) 263-6477.

Referrals from Other Lawyers

Getting referrals from friends or relatives who are lawyers might seem like a good way to find your divorce lawyer, but consider this: lawyers send each other business either because they are friends or because they expect to get paid back with other referrals. Although it's possible that a non-divorce lawyer might refer you to a good divorce lawyer, it's by no means a certainty. If your lawyer friend does not do domestic-relations work, how would he actually know if the other lawyer is any good? The lawyer being recommended may be a good friend but a lousy lawyer. Be skeptical of any referral you obtain from a lawyer unless the referring lawyer has actually been a client of the lawyer being recommended. If your lawyer friend recommends the lawyer that handled his or her own divorce, then place that candidate at the top of your list of attorneys to interview.

The Courthouse

Another place to look for a lawyer is in the records of the courthouse where your divorce case will be litigated. (Usually this will be in the county where you and your spouse live.) When a lawsuit of any kind takes place, be it a criminal case, a contract dispute, or a divorce case, unless the case has been sealed (which is rare), everything that is filed in court becomes public record. Anyone can go to the court where a particular case is pending and read the pleadings and affidavits that have been filed as well as any other records attached to court-filed documents (such as financial statements and medical records). Some courthouses have their domestic or family-law cases separated, either physically or numerically, from other types of cases, and some don't.

You can go to your local courthouse and ask to be given access to the divorce files. Open files are those that are in active litigation; closed files are those that have been litigated to the end or settled. Ask to see both open and closed files. (Older closed files may be stored at a different location.) If you spend some time reading these files, you will notice certain lawyers' names cropping up over and over again. Other lawyers' names will appear only once or twice.

You can read the pleadings in these files, and in some cases you will be able to discern patterns about the lawyers who wrote them. For example, some lawyers represent only men, some represent women only if they are suing for divorce rather than being sued, and some represent only women. Some lawyers write poorly; some write very well. Don't assume that you lack the knowledge or experience to look at these court files. Regardless of your background, you will learn something about the divorce process and divorce lawyers by taking a few hours (or even a few days) to page through court files. You might even be able to enlist the help of a court clerk in your search if you explain what you are doing.

In addition, you might want to go to court several times over a period of a few weeks and visit some hearings and trials. That way you will be able to observe lawyers in action. For example, if you have found a few names of lawyers that interest you in the court files, a clerk may be able to run those names through the court's computer and tell you when their next hearings are. By sitting in the courtroom as a spectator, you will be able to observe anonymously as a lawyer candidate interacts with his or her client before and during a hearing. Such behavior, like a doctor's bedside manner, may prove very important to you. One of my lawyers made a habit of leaving me alone in hearing rooms and courtrooms with my ex-spouse while he went into the hall to talk to the other lawyer. This made me uncomfortable. In contrast, another lawyer of mine was very careful never to leave me alone with my ex. Although this may seem insignificant, the lawyer who never left me alone with my ex-husband was better attuned in general to my needs, and his courtroom manners were just one manifestation of his superior skill.

Paring Down the List

Once you have compiled a list of candidates and collected all the information you can about them, consolidate all your data on the "Lawyer Information Summary Sheet" (Appendix B). You may find that you do not have complete information for all (or for that matter, any) of the candidates. Fill in whatever you have.

Now you need to select four or five lawyers to interview. Delete from consideration—for the time being anyway—the lawyers whom your referral sources said did not return phone calls or maintain good communication. You should also delete lawyers who do not appear to prepare well, those who cannot think on their feet, and those who seem to have taken on too many clients to be able to be effective. Next consider deleting those lawyers who, although technically competent, did not treat their clients with respect. Then delete any lawyers who, according to your sources, lied or billed falsely.

Is there anyone left on your list? If so, that's wonderful. Interview four or five of those lawyers, using the questions for the lawyer listed and explained later in this chapter (page 42). Good luck!

If no lawyers are left on your list, you have two choices. The first is to review the section at the beginning of this chapter on collecting names of lawyers and then try to get more names. Your second choice is one I do not recommend but which may be necessary if the pool of lawyers in your locality is severely limited (which is often the case, since domestic-relations law is not something many lawyers want to do). You might have to choose a few of the least undesirable candidates that you deleted from your original list and interview them while paying careful attention to the negative qualities.

Conducting Interviews

The breakup of a marriage marks the beginning of a new phase in two people's lives when they will no longer rely on or think about each other's feelings as much as before. They will confer less—or not at all—with each other on important issues. Selecting a lawyer may be one of the first big decisions you have made in a long time without consulting your spouse. Depending on the dynamics of your marriage, it may feel quite strange to be making a decision that involves such a large amount of money on your own.

During the interview process, keep in mind that you will be making this decision solely to benefit yourself and, if children are involved, your children. Every lawyer is going to be different, and you may not be compatible with every one you meet. There is no lawyer out there who is right for everyone.

Finding a lawyer is like finding a new car; people have differing needs, tastes, and budgets, and the ultimate selection depends on what you want and what you are willing to pay. The car that fits your needs, tastes, and budget may not be the one your spouse would have chosen. Although you might ask other people how they like the particular car you are considering buying, you probably won't buy it if you don't feel comfortable during your test drive. If the top of your head grazes the ceiling or you can't stand the texture of the upholstery fabric, regardless of how your friends feel about the car, you would trust your own judgment enough not to buy it, wouldn't you?

Hiring a lawyer should be no different. Increasingly, the practice of law has become less of a helping profession and more of a business. Problems with the economy have resulted in the dissolution of many formerly successful law firms. Lawyers flit from firm to firm, making obsolete the concept of loyalty that once reigned in the profession. What this means to you, a potential purchaser of legal services, is that you cannot assume that every lawyer willing to handle your case is competent to do so, even if he or she claims to be. You have to be sufficiently inquisitive and assertive to find out enough about a lawyer to decide whether you can trust your future (and a large portion of your money) to him or her. If a lawyer strikes you as cold, sleazy, passive, obnoxious, distracted—whatever—then you should consider this factor when determining whether to hire him or her. If a lawyer puts pressure on you to hire him or her, or plays hard to get, you must recognize these actions for what they are—sales tactics.

There is no litmus test for finding the right lawyer any more than there is one for finding the right car. If you already know which car you want, it's probably because you've had enough experience driving to know what you like. You'll go after the car you want and pay the price you've decided you can pay without being knocked off course by a salesman. But if this is your first—or even second—divorce, you probably haven't had enough experience with divorce lawyers to recognize one that would be good for you. No matter your level of sophistication, with the interview process described here, you will be able to collect enough information to make the best decision possible.

As you interview the candidates, not only will you learn things about them, but you will also learn things about yourself. Pay attention to your feelings. Which lawyers make you feel better about things and which make you feel worse? As you interview more candidates, you will be able to compare them with each other.

You may be surprised at the wide diversity among the lawyers you interview. You may even experience the disorienting feeling of having two lawyers tell you totally opposite things with equal conviction. But the longer you continue the interview process, the more educated you will become about divorce lawyers and the divorce process, and eventually there will come a time when you decide you have heard enough and are no longer interested in running around to talk to more lawyers. With any luck, this will be when you know whom you want to hire or when you have at least narrowed the field down to a few people you would feel good about hiring.

There may be another lawyer or two that you should consider interviewing even if they are not on your pared-down list. These are lawyers you think your spouse may be considering hiring. Why would you want to interview these lawyers? Because if you interview these lawyers before your spouse consults with them, they will be ethically precluded from representing your spouse by virtue of having already heard confidential information from you and provided you with legal advice. One lawyer cannot represent opposing sides of the same case. Nor can an attorney listen to your side of the story and then turn around and use this confidential information against you by representing your spouse. To do so would constitute an ethical breach known as a "conflict of interest." By interviewing your spouse's candidates before he or she does, you close off your spouse's ability to use those lawyers, even if you eventually decide not to hire any of them yourself.

Once you have compiled a list of candidates and pared it down to a manageable size, it's time to conduct the interviews. Some lawyers will meet with you initially at no charge, while others will charge by the hour. Some attorneys will speak with you by phone for free. If your purpose in interviewing a particular lawyer is mainly to prevent your spouse from hiring him or her, the safest course is to visit that lawyer in person and pay for his or her services by check. That way, you will have proof later (in the form of a canceled check) that you consulted that lawyer and paid him or her for legal advice.

The Lawyer Information Summary Sheet

If you are able to obtain a free telephone consultation, elicit as much information as you can from a candidate over the phone. Remember though: if you want to prevent your spouse from hiring a particular lawyer and you avail your-self of a free telephone interview, you run the risk that the lawyer will not keep any written record of your conversa-tion. If your spouse hires that lawyer, and he or she doesn't recall having spoken with you, you will have no proof.

Before you begin interviewing attorneys, make photo-copies of the "Lawyer Information Summary Sheet" (Appendix B). Enter the information you obtain about each lawyer on a separate form. After speaking with certain can-didates on the phone, it may become apparent to you that you do not want to waste your time going to meet them in person. On the other hand, if, after a telephone conversa-tion, you are still interested in a candidate, set up a face-to-face meeting.

Many (perhaps most) divorce practitioners will charge you a fee for an initial meeting. If you are being charged by the hour to interview a lawyer about his or her qualifica-tions to handle your case, you must maintain control of the interview so that your questions get answered in a reason-able amount of time. Do not permit the lawyer to digress, and once you are satisfied you have the information you need, end the interview—unless you don't mind paying for extra time. Do not assume that because a lawyer is control-ling an interview that the lawyer will not charge you for the time. Generally speaking, a lawyer will charge you for the entire period of time he or she spends with you, whether you are talking about your case, the lawyer's credentials, or the weather.

In all probability, you will be spending a great deal of money on the lawyer you finally choose. Treat the hiring of a lawyer as seriously as you would treat the purchase of a new car; you may eventually spend much more than the price of a new car on your lawyer, and you will have to live with the end result much longer than you would with any car. Treat your interviews of lawyers as job interviews in which you are the would-be boss. Most employers do not hire without checking references, and neither should you. Do not allow a lawyer's attitude that he or she would be doing you a favor by taking you on as a client make you feel you need that particular lawyer. The stress inherent in divorce leads many people to feel desperate and cling to any lawyer. Resist the temptation to do this.

The lawyer who acts self-confident to the point of being arrogant and plays hard to get may be more of a salesperson than a lawyer. The hard-to-get ploy is used by some divorce lawyers to wring outrageous fees out of clients while at the same time treating them badly. This technique is particularly effective on litigants who have been abused by a parent, employer, or spouse and whose self-esteem is impaired as a result. Feeling unworthy to start with, they feel that they do not deserve a good lawyer and that anyone who represents them is doing them a favor.

Just as most job applicants will not knowingly reveal to a prospective employer what their failings are, it is unlikely that the lawyers you interview will highlight their shortcomings. In fact, many lawyers are sufficiently arrogant that they will not even admit that they have any shortcomings. This is why checking references who are not the lawyer's friends or referral sources is vitally important. Even though a lawyer you interview may state unequivocally that your phone calls will not be ignored, the only reliable way to test the truth of that statement is to ask the lawyer's clients if their phone calls were in fact returned. One way to find out the names and addresses of a lawyer's current and former clients is to search the court files for cases in which the attorney has entered an appearance. Many courts can provide you with a computer-generated list of all of a particular lawyer's cases. Once you have the case name and number, you can ask the court personnel to show you the file, which will contain the client's name and address.

If you have a hard time getting hold of a lawyer to make an initial appointment, be on guard. There is a difference between having to wait a few weeks for an appointment (this shows that a lawyer is busy but plans ahead—a good sign) and not being able to get through to make an appointment (this shows that a lawyer is inaccessible—a bad sign).

Questions for the Lawyer and Why You Need to Ask Them

Take a copy of the "Questions for the Lawyer" form (Appendix C) with you to the interview, ask the lawyer the questions on the form, and write down his or her answers. As you listen to the lawyer's answers, consider the reasons for asking each question. Jot down everything about the lawyer that comes to mind as the interview progresses. Later this information will help you remember certain things about the lawyer and help you evaluate his or her suitability for your case.

The questions from the "Questions for the Lawyer" form are reproduced here, followed by the reasons for asking each question and a description of the type of information you are trying to obtain by asking it.

How long have you been practicing law?

How much of your practice is in the field of domestic relations?

Other than domestic relations, what kinds of cases do you handle?

How long have you been doing domestic-relations work?

Are you certified as a specialist in domestic relations?

These questions give you a sense of the lawyer's level of experience. Any lawyer, even one just out of law school, can hang out a shingle. If there is a possibility that any part of your case might be contested, you should try to hire a lawyer who has at least several years' experience in handling domestic cases. Even if a candidate has been practicing law for many years, if he or she does not have experience specifically in domestic-relations law, he or she will not be of much benefit to you. As previously mentioned, some states certify lawyers as specialists in family law if they can demonstrate a certain level of experience in family law and pass a test on it.

Who else, other than you, would be working on my
case and why?

Some lawyers will reel you in as a client and then hand you off to a less-experienced lawyer in the firm to do the actual work. If there is a possibility that this might happen, you need to know ahead of time. It is very frustrating to reach your attorney on the phone only to find out that he or she doesn't know what is going on in your case. In addition, if anyone other than the lawyer you are interviewing will be working on your case, your bill may expand in proportion to the number of people involved. Because this could lead to financial problems, you also need to know about this possibility ahead of time. On the other hand, if a less-experienced lawyer does all the work on your case, your bill may be less than it would have been had the more seasoned lawyer done the same work.

Tell me about three of your cases that were the most
meaningful for you and why.

The answer to this question is not as important as the lawyer's attitude about answering it. Some lawyers may indicate that this is none of your business, or they may not be able to come up with an answer. What you are looking for is a lawyer who will answer this question with passion and conviction. An enthusiastic or an emotion-charged answer demonstrates that the lawyer is not burned out or jaded. You need a lawyer who cares about you not only as a source of income but as a person as well.

> How do you think the local judges perceive you, and which judge do you think is the best to have in a domestic case?

The purpose of this question is not so much to find out how judges perceive the lawyer as it is to find out whether the lawyer cares how judges perceive him or her, and also whether he or she even gets in front of judges often enough for them to have formed an opinion. If the lawyer you are interviewing never gets into court, you will probably hear a very superficial answer to this question. On the other hand, if a lawyer tells you that he or she does well before Judge X but finds Judge Y to be difficult, this is an indication that the lawyer is in court often enough to know who the judges are and what they are like—a good sign. A surprising number of lawyers never get into court and wouldn't recognize the local judges if they met them on the street.

Although courtroom experience is valuable, too-frequent court appearances may signal that a lawyer is unable or unwilling to settle cases. Or he or she may be too over-committed to prepare sufficiently in advance. Clients whose cases should have been settled are forced into going through a trial unnecessarily. For example, if you went to a lawyer tomorrow and said you wanted to sue for divorce, the lawyer could file the papers for you and then do nothing until the trial date arrived. Because your lawyer was not prepared, you would have little settlement leverage. The opposing lawyer, knowing that your lawyer was unprepared, would relish the idea of cleaning up at a trial. Lawyers who are in court every day have very little time to prepare their other cases, which results in many expensive but poor-quality trials.

Ideally, you need an attorney who tries enough cases to be comfortable and effective in court but who also spends enough time on negotiation and preparation to ensure that you won't have to go through a trial unless all the other options have failed.

Beware of any lawyer who, when asked this question, claims to have an "in" with a judge. Such an attorney is unethical and may not be telling the truth. If he or she does actually have an "in" with a judge, something fishy is going on, and both the lawyer and the judge should be reported to the proper authorities.

How do you think the other local domestic-relations lawyers perceive you?

A lawyer who cares too much about what other lawyers think may have a hard time sticking up for your interests. Consider, for example, the case of Sarah and Burt. A judge allotted one hour total to hear the arguments of both of their lawyers. Burt's lawyer went first and took forty-five minutes for his argument. Even though Sarah's lawyer realized he was eating into her time, she didn't speak up when he passed the thirty-minute mark. When Burt's lawyer finally finished, Sarah's lawyer was unable to complete her argument in the fifteen minutes that were left. She noticed a number of other lawyers in the back of the courtroom, waiting for her to finish up so they could have their own cases heard. Fearful of irritating her professional colleagues, she cut her argument short and her client lost.

Such conduct is inexcusable. A lawyer must represent her client's interests zealously. Sarah's lawyer, more interested in getting along with lawyers she sees day in and day out, put her own needs ahead of her client's and may have cost Sarah custody of her child.

Although you want an attorney who demonstrates experience in court, participates in bar association activities, and knows the local customs and procedures, beware of lawyers who are more committed to advancing their reputations with other lawyers than they are to protecting their clients. Probe the lawyer's feelings about his or her role in the local community. Answers that seem to emphasize the lawyer's reputation may signal a narcissism that could prevent a lawyer from placing your needs in the forefront.

Some lawyers think it's OK to act buddy-buddy with the opposing lawyer in their client's presence. Although your lawyer should be cordial and polite to everyone, appearing too friendly with the enemy in front of a client communicates disloyalty and disrespect to the client. It indicates that the lawyer considers his or her professional pursuits more important than the client's needs and feelings. Unfortunately, a great many divorce lawyers find nothing wrong with this behavior. If watching your lawyer chat amiably with opposition counsel would offend you, let lawyer candidates know during your initial interviews. If a candidate dismisses your feelings as invalid, move on to the next candidate.

How often are you in court?
How often are you in court on a domestic-relations matter?

When was the last divorce or custody trial you had?
How long did it take? Who was the judge?
How many open divorce and custody cases do you have
right now?
How many divorce or custody trials have you had in the
past year?
Is there a reason there are so many [or so few]?

A lawyer who has fewer than ten open divorce or custody cases (unless each case is extremely complex) probably
does not do primarily divorce work. This does not necessarily mean that such a lawyer would not be a good one for
you, however. For example, a litigation lawyer who handles
court cases on a number of different subjects besides divorce
would be a viable candidate even with ten or fewer open
divorce cases, as long as he or she had other positive attri-
butes and adequate experience in divorce law. A lawyer who
claims to have fifty or more open cases may be overex-
tended, unless he or she has a number of other attorneys or
paralegals helping out. Remember, though, that it is difficult to generalize about caseloads, so the safest course is to
ask each lawyer about his or her caseload and compare that
with what other lawyers say about theirs. Delete from consideration any attorney who clearly has too much on his or
her plate to take on your problems as well.

Although being in court only rarely may be the mark of
someone who can settle disputes effectively—thereby pre-
venting lengthy and expensive courtroom battles—it also
indicates a lack of courtroom experience. Infrequent court
appearances could mean that a lawyer does not regularly
handle contested matters (not good if your case is contested
by your spouse). On the other hand, if a lawyer is in court
too often—or all the time—he or she may not be able to

focus on issues ahead of time and reach accord via settlement. This could also be a signal that you might have problems contacting the attorney ("I'm sorry, Mr. Eagle is in court all morning") or that the lawyer will not have time to prepare your case before going into court. Look for someone who goes to court regularly but not constantly. A lawyer who handles at least four multi-day divorce or custody trials per year and has done so for the past five years probably has enough trial experience for you to be comfortable with this component of his or her credentials.

Do you represent both men and women? Why or why not?

Do you feel the system works properly to give fair results? If not, what can you do to increase the chances that I will be treated fairly by the system?

A lawyer's answers to these questions will provide you with insight into his or her biases and prejudices. While you don't want a lawyer who is a reactionary zealot, you also don't want one who indiscriminately takes any client who walks through the door as long as he or she pays the bill. Some lawyers are deeply committed to representing only certain types of clients—men, women, people with assets exceeding a certain dollar amount, and so on. If the lawyer you are interviewing does limit his or her practice to certain types of clients, be sure to ask why.

A lawyer who will represent any client who walks through the door or who lacks concern about whether the system operates fairly may run his or her practice like an assembly line. If you want individual attention and quality representation, you need someone with a passion for his or her work and compassion for his or her clients. Listen to the opinions the lawyer voices in response to these questions and see how comfortable you feel with them. Try to determine whether the lawyer will be likely to give you the support, respect, and attention you should expect in exchange for the sizable fees you will be paying.

How often do you handle appeals on behalf of your domestic-relations clients?

How many appeals have you handled in your career?

Handling an appeal is nothing like handling a trial. Appellate lawyers need skills above and beyond what is needed for a trial practice. If a lawyer candidate never or only rarely handles appeals, this is not fatal, but you need to realize that if either you or your spouse appeals after the trial, you will have to find someone else to handle the appeal.

In my opinion, it is better to find a lawyer at the outset who handles both trial and appellate work, for two reasons. First, switching lawyers will require that you spend a lot of money bringing the new lawyer up to speed on what has already happened in your case. And second, appellate lawyers understand how to "preserve the record" for appeal, whereas some trial lawyers do not. What this could mean is that, even if you have a good case on appeal, if your lawyer did not object at the trial, you're out of luck. (The appeals process is described in Chapter 2.)

Two of my lawyers refused or were reluctant to make objections because they were concerned about annoying the judge or not winning the objection. In my opinion, neither of these concerns justified the problems later caused by their failures to preserve my record for appeal.

How much do you charge?

Do you require an advance retainer, and if so, how much is it?

What do you do with the advance retainer? Is a portion of it reserved for the final bill?

How often do you bill?

May I see a sample bill showing what information will be on my bills and the level of detail?

How long after I am billed before payment is due?

Do you take charge cards or offer a payment plan?

What happens if I cannot pay a bill? Do you immediately terminate my representation?

How much do you estimate my case will cost altogether?

What are the terms of the fee agreement?

Unless the lawyer is charging a fixed or contingent fee (which is rare, especially if the case is contested), once you pay your retainer, the bills will start, and they won't stop anytime soon. Although your spouse may eventually be ordered by the court to pay your attorney's fees (if, for example, you earn substantially less or receive substantially less in the divorce), there is no guarantee that this will happen, and your attorney will therefore probably require you to pay the bills yourself as the case progresses. In order for you to understand what you are being charged for, your bills must be very detailed. They must include the date work was performed, an indication of who performed the work, and a detailed description of the type of work performed. Do not accept a monthly statement that says "Work performed, January—$1,800.00." Many lawyers actually get away with this kind of bill. Knowledgeable clients, however, insist on a minute-by-minute explanation of "work." (See Appendix G for a sample bill.)

To understand why a detailed bill is important, consider the case of Sherman, who routinely went over his lawyer's bills as soon as they arrived. On one bill, Sherman found that his lawyer had listed time working on his case during a period that the lawyer had been on vacation. The bill claimed that the lawyer had made some kind of child visitation arrangements, and the lawyer was charging Sherman for this work at his regular hourly rate.

Sherman remembered the incident, which involved a problem the lawyer should have cleared up before leaving on vacation. The lawyer had procrastinated, however, so Sherman wound up having to deal with the problem through the lawyer's secretary. The lawyer then charged Sherman for the secretary's time at the lawyer's hourly rate, claiming that he had done the work himself. When Sherman challenged him, the lawyer admitted the "mistake." Had Sherman not been receiving and reviewing detailed bills, he would have been cheated out of a hundred and fifty dollars or so. Plus he would not have realized what kind of person his lawyer really was.

When the bills start rolling in, you may be amazed at how high they are. (I was, and I'm a lawyer.) What if you simply can't pay? Some lawyers give you ten days and then cut you off. Others will let you get behind a bit. Some accept credit cards, and some will put you on a monthly payment plan. Find out ahead of time if your lawyer will cut you off without mercy. If you really want to hire that lawyer, you will need to make plans for what to do if you run out of money. If you should need to switch lawyers, you will probably have to pay the replacement lawyer a substantial retainer. If you already can't pay one lawyer's bill, how are you going to pay the replacement's retainer? Don't assume that a lawyer will let your bill "revolve" like a credit-card account. Many lawyers will not.

Each candidate you interview should give you a copy of the fee/retainer agreement to read. The terms of your representation should be clear and in writing. (See Appendix E for a "Sample Fee Agreement.") Read the terms and understand them, because once you sign the agreement, you will most likely be bound by its terms. (For more on agreements between lawyers and clients, see Chapter 5: Hiring the Lawyer.)

How long will it be before the case reaches completion?

A lawyer's ability to accurately estimate how long your case will take shows that he or she has enough experience in these matters. You need this information for planning purposes as well. For example, you need to know how long it will be before you can remarry, how long you can expect to be paying legal bills, and how long it will be before you find out whether you will keep or lose your house.

Do you require anything from me in the way of information or otherwise before you can decide whether you can undertake my representation, and if so, what?

A lawyer may give you a list of things he or she needs from you. Or the lawyer or a paralegal may meet with you personally to ask you specific questions. Techniques such as these show that a lawyer is organized and has a tried-and-true method for collecting information from clients. A lawyer who brushes you off by saying, "We'll get to that later, after you've signed the fee agreement and paid the retainer" (or words to that effect) is more focused on making money than doing a quality job for you.

> Have you written any articles or books, given any
> speeches, or taught any classes on domestic-relations
> law? If yes, give details and provide copies of the
> articles.

A lawyer's having written about, lectured about, or taught family law shows a commitment to and an understanding of the law in this field. Just as you would prefer a cardiac surgeon who teaches his technique to medical students over an internist who never performs operations if you were having transplant surgery, so too would you benefit from a divorce lawyer who teaches and writes on the subject as opposed to a general practitioner who handles only one or two uncontested divorces a year.

> What is your rating in *Martindale-Hubbell*?

As discussed earlier in this chapter, the *Martindale-Hubbell Law Directory* contains ratings of lawyers based on the opinions of other lawyers in their geographic area. A lawyer's rating (or lack of one) can be very useful, especially when there is little other information available by which to judge his or her abilities.

> What are your activities in bar association groups
> pertaining to domestic-relations law?

Although lawyers who are active in family-law bar association sections and committees probably know more about family law than lawyers who do not participate, high visibility on bar association sections and committees is not a guarantee that a lawyer will be an effective advocate for you. The self-publicity achieved through these sections and committees may be evidence of an attorney's ability to advocate for him- or herself as opposed to advocating for the interests of his or her clients. Membership in a few sections and committees shows that a lawyer is involved, but too many such activities could indicate that a lawyer has an unchecked need to be needed or an inability to draw the line about taking on responsibilities. It could mean that, once you have paid your retainer, you will be in competition with those activities for your lawyer's time.

> Are you involved in any social causes pertaining to domestic relations (e.g., father's rights, domestic violence issues, lobbying or supporting changes in the law as it pertains to divorce and custody)?

Lawyers committed to causes are often very effective advocates because they actually care about remedying injustice in the system. Lawyers who are involved in causes can sometimes be fanatical, however, or at least be perceived as fanatics by judges. Although you want to find someone to represent you zealously, you need to be wary of lawyers who may have reputations as kooks. You should also make sure that your case lines up with your lawyer's cause. For example, you probably don't want a father's-rights crusader representing you if you're a mother. There are exceptions to every rule, however. If a well-known father's-rights crusader took a mother's case, this fact could be perceived as an indication that the father must really be scum.

> What kind of result do you think we should be looking for in my case, and is this a reasonable goal? Do you feel I have any unrealistic expectations? If so, what are they and why?

These questions should help you determine what a lawyer thinks about your case and whether he or she will fight for your cause. Almost any case is winnable. If a lawyer doesn't think you can get what you want, find out why. It may be that your motives are grounded in revenge rather than reality. On the other hand, it could be that your case, although winnable, is too challenging for that particular lawyer.

How many cases have you had with my spouse's lawyer, and what are your impressions of that lawyer?

Regardless of whether you hire this lawyer, his or her answer to this question will provide you with valuable insights about your spouse's lawyer.

If you are not available to take my call, do you have someone else who will be able to speak with me? If not, how long will it take you to return my call?

A lawyer's accessibility and responsiveness are important. When you have a question, regardless of its urgency, you should be able to get it answered that same day. One of my lawyers was chronically unresponsive, and I tolerated his lack of responsiveness for much too long. I rationalized not hearing from him by thinking that my questions were not as important or urgent as whatever else he was doing. The problem was that, once he ignored my relatively minor questions and less-than-urgent problems for long enough, they became crises.

If a situation is not a problem but will become one in a month if it doesn't get addressed, it still needs attention now. Unfortunately, many lawyers procrastinate about routine matters for so long that these routine matters transform themselves into crises that are either impossible or very expensive to resolve.

Take Nancy's situation, for example. Nancy had agreed with her ex-husband to bring their son to Chicago for a visit every Friday at a specific time, and this agreement was confirmed by a court order. Then her ex-husband's lawyer filed a deposition notice requiring her to be in a town about an hour from Chicago on a Friday at the same time that she had to be in Chicago because of the visit. Nancy was faced with a court order and a deposition notice telling her to be in two different places at the same time. No matter what she did, she would be violating something.

Your lawyer should deal with conflicts like this by calling the other side's lawyer and saying something like, "My client obviously cannot be there then. Why didn't you call me first to set up a mutually agreeable time and place for the deposition?"

Unfortunately, Nancy's lawyer did not pick up on the conflict in her schedule. She called him—no response. She wrote letters—no response. Finally, as the day in question drew near, her lawyer told her that she need not go to the deposition, so she didn't. The other lawyer took advantage of the situation and convinced the judge that either Nancy or her lawyer was flouting the system, and the master ordered Nancy to pay her ex's lawyer fifteen hundred dollars. Because she followed her lawyer's instructions, Nancy was fined fifteen hundred dollars, and her lawyer never apologized or offered to pay.

Don't let yourself become a victim like Nancy. During the early days of my divorce and custody case, contacting my attorney by telephone could consume days. Even though I knew intellectually that my calls should be returned more promptly, I found myself wondering if I was expecting too much. Dissatisfied, I eventually switched lawyers. My current attorneys have been representing me for more than a year, and I cannot recall a single instance when one of my phone calls was not returned the same day, usually within an hour or two. Most of the time I get through the first time I call and do not even have to leave a message. This is the level of responsiveness that all divorce clients should get, but unfortunately the vast majority do not.

> Will you need to hire an expert witness for my case? What will be the areas of expertise and who will you use? How much will this cost?

Many divorce and custody cases will require the involvement of expert witnesses (as discussed in Chapter 2). You need to determine whether the lawyer realizes this and to get a sense of how much an expert will cost. If hiring an expert will exceed the amount you stand to win, it may not be prudent to litigate the case. It is far better to realize this now than a year from now, after having spent thousands of dollars on legal fees.

> What are the different phases of my case? Describe briefly how the process will work.

When you ask this question, you should gain insight into how far ahead your lawyer is thinking and his or her ability to plan. One of the most valuable qualities a lawyer can have is the ability to make a long-term plan and stick with it. Too many lawyers simply react to what the other side is doing and then send you a bill. It is not uncommon for some lawyers to procrastinate until a situation turns into a crisis before doing anything.

If a candidate answers this question with something like, "We can't predict how things are going to turn out," explain that you're not asking him or her to predict a result. Rather, you're asking what the game plan is. A good lawyer will have a strategy in mind. General Schwartzkopf didn't go to the Persian Gulf and wait to see what would happen. He made plans. He made things happen. You need a lawyer who will take control of the case, not a lawyer who will let circumstances and events do the controlling. Listen carefully and try to get an indication whether this person is going to let the other lawyer set the tone or grab hold of the case and make it go the way he or she thinks it should.

My spouse is (or I am) prone to fits of rage and violence. Will this be a factor in my case?

Some lawyers and judges seem to think that domestic violence is no big deal. If your spouse was abusive, the judge may even blame you for it. You absolutely must have a lawyer attuned to this issue. Domestic violence *is* a big deal, and if your lawyer doesn't handle things just right, you could end up a hospital or morgue statistic.

If a candidate glosses over domestic violence and expresses no outrage or sympathy, look elsewhere. On the other hand, if a candidate tells you that the judge is unlikely to consider the domestic abuse issue in a way that will be helpful to you, that lawyer may simply be realistic. Ask if there is a way to get a different judge or how you might win what you're after by using some other strategy. For example, my case involved domestic violence, but the judge seemed to ignore it as a factor in determining custody. So how did I get his opinion overturned? By using a different strategy. We argued that the children should not have been separated. One of the most important qualities a lawyer can have is creativity, the ability to find more than one way to get from Point A to Point B.

Why do you handle divorce cases? Aren't they difficult
  because of all the negative emotion?

The answer to this question will help you figure out
whether a lawyer got stuck doing domestic work because of
an inability to succeed in other areas of law, whether he or
she truly is committed to helping people, or whether he or
she has developed a lucrative racket where clients are
expected to feel grateful for being allowed to be clients. The
ideal candidate is one who handles divorce cases because he
or she wants to help you and because he or she believes his
or her legal skills and experience in this arena will benefit
you, the client.

Have you ever been suspended, disbarred, or
  reprimanded? If yes, give details.
Have you ever been sexually or romantically involved
  with one of your divorce clients?

If a lawyer answers yes to either of these questions, a red
flag should go up. This lawyer may be a good candidate to
avoid. But be aware that not all lawyers will answer these
questions honestly. Even so, you may be able to obtain information about suspensions or disbarments from your local bar
association or attorney disciplinary body.

This whole process of getting a divorce and having to
  testify in court has me really jumpy and nervous. I
  feel like everything is out of control. Is this normal?
  What should I do?

If a candidate seems unwilling to talk to you about emotional problems, this should be cause for concern. It is part
of your lawyer's job to try to understand your feelings and,
to the extent that those feelings are intertwined with your
legal situation, do whatever is possible from a legal stand-

point to help you deal with your feelings. If a lawyer is not prepared to go that distance, then he or she should be practicing in an area of law that is less emotion-laden. On the other hand, you must remember that a lawyer is not a therapist and is trained only to help you with your legal problems.

Some lawyers might suggest that if you are feeling angry, scared, or hopeless, you should see a therapist. Although seeing a therapist may be helpful, it cannot substitute for having an effective, assertive, and strong lawyer who does all that can be done to protect you and advance your cause on the legal battlefield. A therapist cannot protect you from the opposing lawyer's head games, reassure you about the legal strength of your case, or assess the legal risks involved. Only your lawyer can do these things. If a lawyer is not willing to help you deal with the fears and concerns stemming from your legal crisis, he or she is not doing a proper job. A lawyer who is too detached or too busy to deal with the effects that litigation has on your nerves is doing only half a job.

Some sophisticated domestic-relations lawyers, keenly aware of the interplay between their clients' emotional and legal needs, have therapists on staff. This can be a godsend to clients who cannot afford both an attorney retainer and weekly psychotherapy. Such lawyers are few and far between, but if you are emotionally needy or disoriented and fortunate enough to find such a lawyer, hiring him or her may just be the answer to your problems.

Is there anything I haven't asked about that you want to tell me?

This open-ended question encourages the lawyer to open up and give you a peek into his or her personality. An answer like "What types of things do you mean?" shows consideration for you. An answer like "I think you've pretty much covered everything" may belie the attorney's resentment of the interview process and a lack of consideration for you. Whatever the lawyer says or does not say in answer to this question will give you insight into how you feel about this person and how he or she feels about you.

Please give me some references (current or former clients).

If you talk to current or former clients of this lawyer, you will learn how they were treated and how they felt about the quality of the legal representation. This is information you will not be able to find anywhere else. Even though it may seem cumbersome or distrustful, you owe it to yourself to do everything possible to weed out the bad lawyers. A lawyer may not be able to disclose his clients' names without checking with them first. However, the information is worth waiting for. Tell the lawyer you will call back in a few days to get the references. You may also be able to obtain names of a lawyer's clients from your local courthouse's computer system (see pp. 33–35).

4

Finding the Right Lawyer for You

Analyzing the Information

After each interview, review the lawyer's responses and complete the "Lawyer Information Summary Sheet" (Appendix B). Using the information you obtained from interviews to select your lawyer is a three-step process that consists of (1) weeding out the unsuitable lawyers, (2) determining the best of those who remain by using the checklist called "The Top Ten Qualities to Look for in a Divorce Lawyer" (see page 75), and (3) applying a "Smell Test" (see page 76). Attorneys often behave differently when they are trying to woo you as a client than they will after you have paid a retainer. Because of this, the signs of bad lawyering are sometimes hidden until after you have hired the lawyer. Once your lawyer's true colors begin to show, you might also need to use the guidelines in this chapter to help you decide whether to fire your lawyer and find a new one.

Listening to Your Instincts

You can weed out unsuitable candidates because they fit the profile of one of the "Lawyers to Avoid" (described beginning on page 65) or because there is something about them that you just don't like. Weeding out is a very subjective process: only you can know if you and a particular lawyer will "click." You must therefore learn to trust your instincts as you go through this process.

For example, think about whether a lawyer made eye contact with you, and if not, whether this bothers you. Was the lawyer glib, dismissive, or callous? Did he or she oversimplify the issues or make you feel your cause was hopeless? Did you hear any words of encouragement, or did you only hear about how wonderful the lawyer considers him- or herself? Factors such as these—and your reactions to them—are legitimate considerations when choosing an attorney. Do not overlook behaviors you find offensive and hope that they will go away. They won't.

Lawyers who handle divorces come in all shapes and sizes. There are those rare, kind souls who live to help their clients by providing psychological and legal support during a stressful period in their lives. But then there are those who see divorce as a relatively simple, mechanical process that generates income; those who punish and bully their clients' spouses because of their own unresolved personal problems; and those who, unable to succeed in another area of the law not so fraught with negative emotion, are stuck doing divorces for a living.

Lawyers, like other people, have their own individual personalities and problems. Nothing distinguishes a lawyer from the rest of humanity except the act of having gone to law school and passing the bar exam. Like any other person, a lawyer can be disorganized, careless, irresponsible, overcommitted, vengeful, greedy, addicted, or otherwise undesirable. Like any other person, a lawyer can have ideological perceptions totally different from your own. No state licensing board has screened out undesirable or incompatible lawyers. This is your job, and you must do it while enduring the pain of divorce. It won't be easy. It will take guts. But by doing your homework, you should be able to make an educated choice about the lawyer who will play a very important role in how you will live the rest of your life.

Lawyers to Avoid

Be on the lookout for behavior that indicates the following lawyers to avoid. If one of the behaviors listed here came through during an interview, cross the name of that lawyer off your list.

The Overcommitted Lawyer

Divorce lawyers make money based on how much time they can bill. The more cases they have, the more opportunity they have to bill. This is why divorce lawyers sometimes take on too many cases. Rather than focusing on doing a good job for the clients they already have, they become preoccupied with building up a stockpile of cases to increase their own wealth. This affects clients negatively by making the lawyer hard to reach by phone. Overcommitment can also make it difficult for a lawyer to attend to small problems early enough to prevent them from turning into crises. Because the clients of an overcommitted lawyer are the victims of so many dire emergencies that only the lawyer can take care of, this type of lawyer can develop an exaggerated sense of self-importance which can result in your being belittled when you need him or her to take care of a relatively small concern. The overcommitted lawyer's m.o. in such a situation will be to ignore your requests for help until you have a crisis on your hands, at which time your concerns will be addressed, but at higher cost to you because a crisis is more time-consuming to deal with than a minor problem.

An overcommitted lawyer often has employees or co-workers who can help with the overload. Sometimes this solves the problem, and sometimes it makes things worse. When an overcommitted lawyer delegates work to someone else, especially if that someone else is a less-experienced attorney, the inexperienced lawyer can make mistakes that the overcommitted lawyer won't catch because he or she is busy working on other things.

Knowing how many open cases a lawyer has and how many people he or she has available to help can help you determine if a lawyer is overcommitted. Another test of whether a lawyer is overcommitted is how easily you can reach his or her office by telephone and have a problem solved or question answered. When all you get is the runaround, no matter how well intentioned the lawyer is, your interests are not being protected. Do yourself a favor and do not commit your future to an already overcommitted lawyer.

The Disorganized or Distracted Lawyer

A lawyer who is disorganized or easily distracted is a disaster waiting to happen. In the legal world, a missed deadline can be catastrophic. A good lawyer is aware of all pending deadlines and to-do items imposed by the court and the other side. He or she gets things done on time while simultaneously developing and implementing strategies to get you what you deserve. A lawyer who cannot return phone calls promptly, provide accurate bills, or conduct a meeting without allowing interruptions may not be sufficiently organized to advance your interests. Not returning calls, arriving late for meetings, messy piles of papers and files, a harried staff, an inability to make uninterrupted time available to you reasonably soon after you request it—these are all signs that a lawyer may be disorganized and should be weeded out.

The Passive Lawyer

It may be hard to weed out the passive lawyer because he or she seems so calm and relaxed. Being around a passive lawyer can make you feel good because the lawyer doesn't seem to be worried about anything. The passive lawyer answers your questions with generalities that minimize the seriousness of your concerns. The problem is, the passive lawyer doesn't take anything very seriously, including the consequences to you if your case is not handled well. The passive lawyer tends to react to what your spouse's lawyer wants and forgets that he or she is supposed to pursue your case assertively. The passive lawyer calls to tell you when you need to gather documents or answer questions for the other side but is slow to turn the tables and make the other side gather documents and answer questions for you. Lacking a sense of urgency, the passive lawyer waits until the last minute to start on work and then does a half-baked job because there isn't enough time to do it well. The passive lawyer is unable to get enough adrenaline pumping to be a champion for anyone.

The Assembly-Line Lawyer

Lawyers who practice assembly-line law treat every case exactly the same, and every case moves along like a part on a conveyor belt. Like assembly-line workers, assembly-line lawyers do not apply creative problem-solving skills to their work because their work consists simply of repeating the same set of movements over and over again. Like assembly lines in general, assembly-line lawyers can be efficient and economical in some circumstances. But if your case involves a contested divorce or custody fight, complex financial issues, or anything else out of the ordinary, you should weed out assembly-line lawyers. If, however, you and your spouse agree on everything and simply need a lawyer to memorialize your agreement in legally binding form, an assembly-line lawyer may be just the ticket. Such lawyers handle these matters routinely and will have pre-drafted forms available that will save you much time and money.

The Bully

As most schoolchildren know, every playground has its bully. Instead of eventually learning to get along, some bullies grow up to become lawyers who view their law licenses as permits to be deliberately obnoxious and harassing. Being a courtroom lawyer is perceived by these people as a socially acceptable way to live one's life as a bully.

I write about the bully here because many people desirous of an amicable divorce are inclined to automatically weed out the bully. But if your spouse's lawyer is a bully or your spouse is a bully (or both of them are), you must hire your own bully. Taking the high road—being fair and ethical—will not protect you against the tactics of the bully. If you offer to split everything fifty-fifty, you can be sure the bully will never settle for that. Once the bully knows what is agreeable to you, come hell or high water, he or she will make sure you get less. The bully is so tenacious and emotionally vested in depriving you of whatever you are willing to settle for that—unless you have your own bully who understands this mentality and knows how to turn it against the other side—you will be worn down to nothing, financially and emotionally, before the divorce is over.

The worst kind of lawyer you can have if your spouse or your spouse's lawyer is a bully is a lawyer who constantly advocates compromise. Such a dynamic is similar to when marriage counselors tell the wives of abusive men that "it takes two to have an argument." If you buy into this logic, you will lose all your money, all your children, and all your self-esteem. The more you give in to the bully, the more he or she will expect you to give in. You need a lawyer who can make it clear that, not only will you not allow yourself to be bullied, but until the bully stops, you are going to be a bully right back. In sum, if there is a bully on the other side, your lawyer needs to be one, too.

Judges, mediators, social workers, and psychologists involved in divorce often advocate the idea that parents must get along with each other for the benefit of their children. They often consider any parent who can't get along with the other the disfavored parent in a custody battle. Some states even have laws, called "friendly parent" provisions, that allow the court to consider a parent's willingness to have joint custody as one reason to award custody to that parent. Some judges believe that it is within a parent's power to get along simply by giving in. Give in, though, and you will have heightened conflict and more bullying to look forward to. You cannot look to judges or court-appointed mediators or psychologists for help. They will simply apply pressure to both of you to work things out. What you need is someone to apply pressure to the bully, and the only person who can do that is your lawyer.

The Liar

Another stereotypical divorce lawyer is the liar, who can stand in front of a judge and spit out lies so fast your head starts to spin. This type of lawyer says whatever will advance his or her immediate goals, regardless of whether it is true. For example, to appear conciliatory and curry favor with a judge, the liar will promise to sign a certain agreement but later, when actually presented with the paper, will refuse to do so. Although it can be comforting to have someone on your side who will say or do anything to get you what you want, lying lawyers are not above lying to their clients. Moreover, lying lawyers are sometimes preceded by their reputations, and judges and other lawyers don't trust them. Hook up with a lying lawyer and you may be found guilty by association: the judge may be inclined not to believe anything *you* say.

What if your spouse is represented by a liar? Your only hope is to find yourself a lawyer with a mind like a steel trap who can keep track of the lies and throw them back in the liar's face, a lawyer who is organized and compulsive enough to get everything from the liar in writing. Unfortunately, this level of commitment and attention to detail is rare in divorce lawyers. What's worse, if you complain to your lawyer that he or she lets your spouse's lawyer get away with too many lies, then you risk creating an adversarial relationship with your own lawyer. Which brings us to yet another type of lawyer.

The Defensive Lawyer

When you express concern to your lawyer about your case or the way he or she is handling it, the defensive lawyer may say (or imply) that you need not worry about such details.

This is not unlike a doctor telling the patient who suffers from a malady he or she cannot diagnose that it is all in the patient's head. If you are critical of your lawyer, you may find that, rather than correcting the problem, the lawyer becomes defensive by attacking you. By carefully screening your lawyer candidates, you can weed out those who would rather lay a guilt trip on you for being demanding than work a little harder themselves.

Consider the divorce case of Joan and Bob. Joan agreed to give Bob two-thirds of her pension in order to settle the case, mainly because she wanted to stop fighting and get on with her life. Bob had a long history—during the marriage and the divorce—of agreeing to things and then changing his mind later (or forgetting what he had agreed to). Joan was afraid that Bob would take the money and then come back later asking for more. She expressed this concern to her lawyer, who observed, "He won't have a leg to stand on if he tries to do that." But Joan knew that not having a leg to stand on had never before stopped Bob from making a run at whatever he wanted. She told her lawyer she wanted a written release from Bob, agreeing not to ask for any more money once he got his agreed-upon share. Her lawyer wrote a letter to Bob's lawyer asking for a release.

Bob ignored the requests for a release and kept asking for his money, but Joan, trusting her instincts, refused to give it without first getting the release. Joan's lawyer became exasperated with her for making things more complicated than they needed to be and told her she didn't need a release. Joan told her lawyer that, if he did not think she needed a release, she would follow his advice and give Bob the money. However, before doing so, she asked the lawyer for his written agreement to represent her for free if Bob came back asking for more money. Joan pointed out that, if her position was as strong as her lawyer maintained, there would be no risk of him having to represent her for free because Bob would not be coming back for more. At this point, Joan's lawyer got busy and drafted the release, which Bob signed because he wanted the money.

This story had a happy ending, but Joan shouldn't have had to fight so hard to get her lawyer to prepare a release protecting her. Why didn't her lawyer come up with the idea of a release on his own? Why did Joan have to involve her lawyer's personal finances to make him focus on the fact that he was creating a risk for her by not getting the release? Many divorce lawyers just go through the motions, send their clients bills, and don't spend much time focusing on what they could do to make the process easier or quicker for their clients. And these lawyers have no regrets about profiting from the misfortune of their clients. After all, the defensive lawyer rationalizes, if clients don't want to spend the money on lawyers, they can always stop litigating; if they want to keep fighting, let them pay.

Perhaps this selfish and shortsighted thinking can be excused as a consequence of being bombarded with too much negative emotion. Just as a doctor cannot get emotionally involved with every terminal cancer patient, a divorce lawyer can't really become overly concerned about the welfare of his or her warring clients. The lawyer's job is to get the client divorced. How well the client fares in the process and how much it costs, psychically and financially, are issues many divorce lawyers have given themselves the luxury of not worrying about.

The "What do you want *me* to do about it?" Lawyer

Another classic divorce lawyer is the "What do you want *me* to do about it?" lawyer. Whenever a tough problem looms—

or even a not-so-tough problem—this type of lawyer asks the client, "What do you want me to do?" In this way, the lawyer hands the responsibility for strategizing the case (which is the lawyer's job, of course) to the client. That way, if the client is not happy with the result, the lawyer can say, "Well, I did what you told me to do, so it's not my fault." This kind of thing tends to happen at times of crisis or at crucial moments in the litigation—times when emotions are running high and the lawyer begins to feel that he or she might be losing control. Although it is difficult to determine in advance whether a candidate is this type, once a lawyer has begun working on your case, the tendency is easy to spot and may be serious enough to consider a change of attorney.

Suppose you are in a meeting with your ex and both of the lawyers, and you have just about worked out a custody and visitation schedule that everyone can agree to. If the agreement goes through, a hearing scheduled for next week will not be necessary. Just at the moment when agreement seems to have been reached and everyone is about to get up and leave, your spouse says, "I won't agree to this unless my ex-spouse gives me back the engagement ring." You are shocked. You don't want the deal to fall through, but the ring could be valuable and you wanted your daughter to have it when she gets married. Your head is spinning. You can't just give in, but it seems that if you don't, the carefully crafted deal you almost had will fall through. This is where your lawyer should step in. A pox on the lawyer who looks at you and says, "What do you want me to do?" If this happens to you, take your lawyer to a private location and ask, "What do *you* recommend?" Then, when the immediate crisis is over, think long and hard about whether this lawyer is doing you any good.

If your lawyer makes a habit of asking you what to do, he or she is either incompetent or trying to get rid of you. I have a friend whose divorce lawyer was totally stymied by the lawyer on the other side. My friend's lawyer was quite simply in over her head, but she was unable to admit this to herself or to my friend. Rather than offer to help my friend find another lawyer, rather than admit she was out of her league, here is what this lawyer did: every time the opposing lawyer sent a letter or filed a pleading, my friend's lawyer would photocopy it and attach a yellow stickie that said "Please advise." She would then send this packet to my friend who, if she had known what to do, would not have needed to hire a lawyer in the first place. This kind of situation is not unlike a plumber coming to your home to fix a clogged toilet and then asking you how you expect him to fix it.

Sometimes divorce lawyers also inform you that if you had not married your spouse, you would not be in your current predicament. To continue the plumbing analogy, this is not unlike the plumber telling you that if you had not put the offending item down the toilet, it would not be stopped up. So you stopped up the toilet! That doesn't mean the plumber doesn't have to figure out how to unclog it if he or she expects to get paid.

A lawyer asking a client "What do you want me to do?" is not the same as asking a client to make a choice or a decision. For example, your lawyer cannot decide substantive issues for you, such as whether you are satisfied with visitation every other weekend or satisfied with getting the station wagon instead of the Jeep. These are decisions you must make. But if you tell your lawyer you want half the savings account and the Jeep, your lawyer should not ask you how to go about getting them. That's a lawyer's job.

The Substance Abuser

Lawyers are not immune to alcoholism or drug abuse. Some would even argue that lawyers in high-stress practice areas such as family law are more prone to alcohol and substance abuse than other professionals. Don't assume that because a lawyer has nice clothes or a fancy office that he or she couldn't be an alcoholic or drug addict. A lawyer who is a substance abuser will probably not admit it to you (or even to him- or herself), but if you have suspicions based on what others have told you—or the lawyer's own behavior, mannerisms, physical appearance, or odor—weed this person out. You have enough problems without adding an addicted lawyer to the list.

The Top Ten Qualities to Look for in a Divorce Lawyer

Once you have weeded out the undesirable lawyers, you can move into the next phase of selecting your lawyer. Using the information you have gathered, rate the remaining candidates on a scale of one to five in each of the following ten categories. Seriously consider the lawyer who scores the highest as your front-running candidate.

1. Will this lawyer act rather than react?
2. Will this lawyer control my case instead of letting the lawyer on the other side, or the judge, control things?
3. Is this lawyer knowledgeable enough about the law and astute and adept enough to use his or her knowledge to control the judge?
4. Does this lawyer have credibility with the judge and other lawyers?

5. Will this lawyer plan ahead by devising and implementing a long-range strategy for success that includes contingency plans?
6. Will this lawyer treat me with respect, care about how I feel, and help me through this process?
7. Will this lawyer return my phone calls promptly?
8. Will this lawyer refuse to be intimidated by anyone, including judges and other lawyers?
9. Will this lawyer be cost-conscious and not spend my money without a compelling reason?
10. Will this lawyer be a zealous champion of my interests?

The Smell Test

Once you have scored the candidate using the "Top Ten" checklist, complete your analysis by applying what I like to call the "smell test." Take a whiff of each lawyer—figuratively speaking—and see if you like what you smell. Do you feel comfortable with this person? Do you feel that he or she is strong enough and aggressive enough to protect you and intimidate the other side's lawyer? Why is this important?

A divorce—like a tennis game, a contested election, or a war—involves strategy and psychology. One side can create a tactical advantage by making the other side feel hopeless, defensive, or exhausted. Many divorces, including those that start out amicably, involve these types of mind games. For example, at various points during the divorce process, you may have to listen to the other side drone on about how you are going to lose (or do not deserve) your house or your children or your savings. This will be so scary and unpleas-

ant that you may feel like giving up, running away, or taking matters into your own hands. You need a lawyer who can
put things in perspective for you and reassure you if the
other lawyer is just posturing. You also need a lawyer who
can posture back and strike fear into your spouse as effectively as this is being done to you.

Take Lisa's case, for example. Lisa had a lawyer who
called her whenever the other side was trying a new tactic.
"Lisa, we've got big problems," she would say. Although the
lawyer may have felt that way, it was not appropriate for her
to communicate that tone of desperation to Lisa, her client.
A lawyer should assess a situation and then inform the client
of it in an objective and emotionally neutral tone. For example, Lisa's lawyer could have said, "The other side has filed
a motion to freeze your assets. If it succeeds, you will not
have access to your checking account. While I think there
is only a twenty-five percent chance they will succeed, we
need to take certain steps, and this is what I recommend we
do . . ." A phone call like that would have been much more
productive and reassuring than the call Lisa received.

Lisa's story may sound far-fetched, but some lawyers
actually act that way. Just as you would steer clear of a doctor who, upon observing your broken leg, said, "We've got
big problems," you should avoid such lawyers as well. Why
would a lawyer behave in ways that make a client feel
uncomfortable, uncertain, and afraid? Perhaps the lawyer is
painting a picture of doom so that, regardless of what happens in the end, he or she looks like a hero for getting a good
result. Or a lawyer may be trying to dispel unrealistic expectations on the part of the client. Or a lawyer who really has
no idea what to do might simply be doing a bad job of
masking his or her own feelings of hopelessness. Or perhaps
a lawyer wants to keep the client in a position of sub-

servience or dependence in order to feed his or her own need to feel needed or in control. Although this last reason may sound extreme, some states have actually found it necessary to prohibit sexual relationships between lawyers and clients, presumably because lawyers were preying on clients who were suffering the emotional trauma of divorce. If you get "vibes" from your lawyer (or lawyer candidates) that such a dynamic might come into play, trust your feelings and give that person a wide berth.

Don't automatically assume that lawyers are qualified and able to do a good job. Just as you will find shoddy merchandise in stores, you will find lousy lawyers behind desks. Lawyers come with problems just the same as the rest of us. As tempting as it might be to blindly trust the first lawyer who agrees to take your money, *don't do it!* Keep looking until you find someone who can help you feel better about your situation—someone who actually has a plan to make your situation better. *You're entitled!*

5

Hiring the Lawyer

Your interviews are complete. You've reviewed all your notes and analyzed all the information you've compiled, and you think you know whom you want to hire. What next?

Reading the Contract

If the lawyer you're considering hiring didn't provide you with a copy of his or her standard contract at your interview, you should ask for one now. This document, commonly referred to as a "fee agreement" or "retainer agreement," will spell out the terms of your relationship with your lawyer. It should describe how you will be charged, what you will be charged for, what the billing rates will be, what the lawyer proposes to do, and what the lawyer expects you to do. If the lawyer anticipates billing you for things other than his or her time—such as postage, photocopying, computerized legal research, expert witnesses, detectives, word processing, travel expenses, and so on—these should be spelled out in the fee agreement. A sample fee agreement appears in Appendix E. Some lawyers' fee agreements are much more detailed than others, and the level of detail in a lawyer's fee agreement does not necessarily correlate with how well a lawyer will handle a case.

If a lawyer has no fee agreement to show you, a red flag should go up. Many jurisdictions require lawyers to have written fee agreements with clients, but even if your jurisdiction does not, it is still necessary for you to understand your and your lawyer's rights and obligations. These should be spelled out in writing at the beginning of your relationship so neither client nor lawyer can claim a misunderstanding later.

Take Jerome's situation, for example. He located Lawyer X after a lengthy search and hired him primarily because he felt comfortable with him. Jerome trusted Lawyer X and, unlike most of the other lawyers he had interviewed, he had no trouble talking to him or understanding him. Lawyer X told Jerome that he charged an hourly rate of $150 but said no written fee agreement was necessary. The lawyer sent Jerome a letter thanking him for retaining him to represent Jerome in his "domestic-relations matter" and requesting a retainer of $7,500. Feeling they understood each other, Jerome gave Lawyer X the retainer.

As the case progressed, Jerome continued to feel that his initial impression had been correct. His attorney appeared to be a warm, caring, down-to-earth man who always found time to answer Jerome's questions and keep him fully informed of all developments in the case. Whenever Jerome was faced with choices that were difficult, whenever he wasn't sure what to do, he felt comfortable relying on his lawyer's recommendations.

Unfortunately, Jerome's divorce did not go as smoothly as his relationship with his lawyer seemed to. Three years later and the retainer long gone, Lawyer X was still hard at work on Jerome's behalf. Lawyer X explained that Jerome's wife had hired a snake-in-the-grass lawyer who made the entire divorce process take much longer than necessary. After Jerome's retainer was used up, his lawyer began sending detailed monthly bills, which Jerome reviewed carefully and then juggled his budget to pay. One month, Jerome noticed that he was being billed at $200 per hour instead of the usual $150. Assuming a clerical error, Jerome contacted his attorney, who informed him that he had raised his rates.

Jerome was flabbergasted. Could a lawyer just all of a sudden do that? What could Jerome do? Start over with a new lawyer? Even though Jerome understood the concept of inflation, having his already-costly legal fees increase so much with no notice left a bad taste in his mouth. He couldn't help but wonder whose best interest Lawyer X had in mind. He started wondering whether his case had dragged on so long because of his wife's snake-in-the-grass lawyer or because his own attorney wanted to continue billing him. The trust he had once felt for his lawyer started slipping away, and Jerome began to second-guess almost all of the recommendations his lawyer had made so far. His sense of security was replaced with paranoia, and Jerome was left wondering if there was anyone he could trust.

It is not improper—or unusual—for a lawyer to periodically raise his or her rates (unless the lawyer has specifically agreed not to). If Jerome had obtained a written contract from Lawyer X, it most likely would have provided either that the hourly rate would last for the duration of the representation or that it would not. Either way, Jerome would have known what was coming and could have dealt with the issue when he signed the fee agreement. Any price hikes could have been anticipated and taken in stride instead of coming as an unwelcome shock.

An attorney should routinely supply a written fee agreement at the initial interview. If a lawyer does not provide one, you should insist on it. Not putting the fee agreement in writing is almost certain to create misunderstandings that will eventually erode what could have been a good lawyer-client relationship.

Once you review the fee agreement, you may wonder whether you can find a lawyer who will charge you a flat fee or a contingent fee instead of billing you by the hour. A lawyer will not usually quote a flat fee for a contested divorce because there is no way to anticipate how complicated such a case will become. If your divorce is not contested, you and your spouse may be able to find lawyers to handle it for a flat fee. If a lawyer quotes you a flat fee and you think your spouse will contest the divorce, make sure you have a clear understanding—in writing—about what is and is not covered by the flat fee.

A contingent fee arrangement provides that the lawyer does not get paid unless the client recovers money, in which case the lawyer gets a portion of it. Contingent fees are common in cases where an injured client is unable to pay a lawyer but a relatively large recovery is anticipated. Generally speaking, contingent fee arrangements are prohibited in divorce cases because lawyers working on a contingent fee basis would not be paid if their clients reconciled. Such lawyers might therefore be tempted to discourage a reconciliation even if it was in their clients' best interests. As a result, courts and legislatures generally do not allow lawyers to provide services to divorce clients on a contingent fee basis.

If you have any questions about what the contract means, ask the lawyer. Do not sign an agreement you do not understand. If you have a problem with specific provisions in the contract, ask the lawyer if they can be changed. Many times they can be. If, however, a lawyer says that something must be in the contract but he or she won't hold you to it, *beware*. Such an attorney may not be ethical. Aside from treating clients poorly, a lawyer who is known to be unethical may also have a difficult time gaining trust or cooperation from adversaries, which could result in your case being more complicated and expensive.

Take Sandy's case. A hearing was scheduled to determine where the children would spend Thanksgiving. Sandy and her ex were able to reach agreement before the hearing, however, so Sandy told her lawyer to call off the hearing. Her lawyer wanted to, but the lawyer representing Sandy's ex was known for going back on his agreements. Sandy's lawyer told her, correctly, that in order to fully protect her rights, he would have to get a written stipulation from the other side before he could call off the hearing. Unfortunately, the stipulation could not be drafted quickly enough, and both attorneys had to go to court on the day of the hearing. If Sandy's lawyer had been able to trust the opposing lawyer, an extra expense to both sides could have been avoided. Doubts about the credibility of the other lawyer prevented Sandy's lawyer from taking any shortcuts. When a "bad apple" is representing one of the litigants, distrust leads to extra expense for everyone involved.

Your first opportunity to find out if a lawyer you are considering hiring might be unethical will be in the initial interview, when you discuss the terms of the fee agreement and representation. If a lawyer seems shifty, inconsistent, glib, unwilling to answer your questions directly, or otherwise untrustworthy, it is a safe bet that other attorneys will perceive him or her that way, too. You are probably better off hiring someone else.

Understanding the Financial Terms

Be sure you understand the financial terms a lawyer is offering you. It comes as a shock to many legal customers when they learn that they are billed by the minute for talking on the phone to their lawyer and for their lawyer's talking on the phone to the other side's lawyer. Billing in this manner is the norm. It is how lawyers earn a living. Think of it as being similar to a store's inventory. Just as a store does not give away merchandise, lawyers do not give away their time. Some attorneys bill by the precise amount of time spent, while others bill in fifteen- or twenty-minute increments. Even if your lawyer spends three minutes reading a note you sent him, he may bill you for his fifteen-minute minimum. If a fee agreement does not address the issue of increments, ask the attorney about it and consider adding language to the agreement to cover this point. Treat the fee agreement the lawyer proposes as a starting point, not a final document. If it contains things you don't like or is missing things that are important to you, talk to the lawyer about making the appropriate additions and deletions before you sign it.

You should also find out what you will be charged for in addition to the lawyer's time. Will you be charged for postage, photocopies, long-distance telephone calls, faxes, expert witness fees, detective fees, supplies, travel expenses, courier fees, computerized legal research, or anything else extra? Remember, lawyers routinely charge for these extras, and these costs can mount up quickly. For example, some lawyers charge twenty-five cents for each photocopy they make or five dollars for each fax they send or receive. These extras are typically itemized in the fee agreement. If they are not, find out what each charge will be, and ask the lawyer to estimate how much they will cost you each month so that you can be prepared for the bill when it arrives. A lawyer will not be able to quote you an exact figure because future expenses are impossible to predict and depend to a large extent on how the other side conducts its case. The lawyer should, however, be able to give you a rough estimate of a range of monthly expenses you should expect to incur.

If a particular charge seems excessive (the per-page rate for photocopies, for example), discuss it with the attorney. Perhaps an adjustment can be made. If not, at least you will have learned of the issue ahead of time and can choose a different lawyer if the problem is significant enough.

If you hire this lawyer, will other people in the office, such as paralegals and secretaries, be working on your case? If so, at what rates will their work be billed? In many cases, paralegal work will be billed at a rate lower than the attorney's, and secretarial work will not be billed at all. If this is the case, you can control your costs to some extent by talking with a secretary or paralegal about certain issues instead of speaking directly with the attorney. You might want to consider meeting with the other people who will be working on your case before you hire a lawyer.

In some firms, certain lawyers are the "rainmakers" who bring in the business, while others do the legal work. The rainmakers are like car salespeople, and the lawyers who do the work are like the service department. The friendly, fatherly rainmaker who lures you in as a client may not be the one who does the actual work on your case. On the other

hand, you may find that you relate better to the young asso-
ciate assigned to your case than to the lawyer you originally
thought you were hiring. Moreover, the younger lawyer's
hourly rate will usually be lower. Even so, you may not
appreciate having your case handed off to an inexperienced
stranger. That's why it's a good idea to find out before you
sign a contract who will actually be doing the work on your
case.

Beware of any language in the fee agreement that gives
a lawyer a "lien" or other right to your house or other assets.
Such language could entitle your lawyer to encumber your
house or bank accounts. Also be wary of language that permits a lawyer to obtain a "confessed judgment." This could
enable your lawyer to sue you for unpaid fees and win automatically without your being able to put on a defense.

Obtaining an Action Plan

Once your marital problems have risen to the level of a court
case with lawyers involved, you will find yourself feeling like
a passenger in a small rubber raft, floating with the current.
At first, the current may be slow or even stagnant. At times,
there will be storms that stir up the current. You will never
know from one day to the next what the current will be like
or where it will take you. You know you are headed for a
waterfall—trial—but you don't know where it is, how to
avoid it, or what to do once you get there.

Only one person can rescue you from any dangers up
ahead, and that is your lawyer. A truly effective lawyer will
harness the energy of the river and use it to steer your raft
to a quiet pond where rational thought is possible and an
agreement can be reached about how everyone can avoid
going over the waterfall. But this cannot happen if your

lawyer does not do careful advance planning. Your lawyer might hop in the raft with you, tell you about the waterfall up ahead, and furiously bail water, but will such frantic efforts prevent you from going over the falls? If a lawyer has no plan but simply reacts to the other side (or to the legal system's time deadlines), it may appear as if the lawyer is doing work even though he is very ineffective.

This is why—*before* you hire a lawyer—you should have a very clear and detailed understanding of what he or she proposes to do in order to win your custody and divorce case. I refer to this as the *action plan*. The action plan should be a detailed listing of everything the lawyer intends to do to further your interests in the litigation. The action plan should include not only a list of all planned activities but also deadline dates for completing these tasks. The action plan should also, where appropriate, show alternatives in case the initial plan fails. Suppose your lawyer plans to seek emergency relief to place your child in your custody instead of your spouse's. What happens next will depend on how the emergency motion is resolved. Thus, the action plan should contain two plans for what to do after the emergency hearing—Plan A for if you win, and Plan B for if you lose. It may take the attorney several hours to prepare such a plan, and you should be prepared to pay for this time.

You may meet with some resistance when you request an action plan from your lawyer. He or she may say, "I cannot predict the outcome of your case or what will happen along the way." Although it is true that no lawyer can predict an outcome, the fact remains that your lawyer must have a game plan to be effective.

Some attorneys are so organized that they have pre-printed forms and form letters for all the stages of different kinds of cases. An action plan is a routine part of the service they provide all their clients. For example, attorney Charles Robertson of Dallas, Texas, gives each new client a free, one-hundred-page, leather-bound and gold-embossed *Client's Handbook to Divorce*. Likewise, Tennessee attorney Larry Rice recommends in his book *The Complete Guide to Divorce Practice* (Chicago: American Bar Association, 1992) that clients be provided with written materials, a booklet, or a videotape describing the legal system. A lawyer who provides written or taped materials to educate you about what can and will happen thereby demonstrates his or her organizational and planning skills.

Many lawyers, however, do not have a systematic approach. Rather, they deal with each case individually— from scratch. This in and of itself is not a contraindication for hiring a lawyer, but if the lawyer doesn't want to focus on your case long enough to map out a strategy at the very beginning, then his or her attention may be too fragmented to do a good job for you. If the lawyer hesitates to give you what you are asking for, make sure you are making yourself clear. Tell the lawyer you don't want any predictions or guarantees. You simply want to know how he or she plans to win your case—in writing.

If the lawyer tries to persuade you that preparing such a plan now would be premature, ask why. Since you have not yet retained this lawyer, you are in the strongest bargaining position you will ever be in. Once you have paid the retainer, you will have a vested interest in staying with the lawyer. Before you hire the lawyer, though, the lawyer is still trying to woo you as a client. If a lawyer is not willing to put in the time, thought, and effort necessary to plan your effective representation before he or she has your business, why would he or she be inclined to do so once your hefty retainer has been deposited? You are paying for the lawyer's time, so there should be no reason for him or her to balk at preparing such a document. If a lawyer is unwilling to do it, seriously consider not hiring him or her.

You *must* obtain an action plan when you hire a lawyer. Corporations, insurance companies, and other litigation-savvy clients insist on detailed proposals and projected budgets from their outside lawyers and then monitor the case to make sure that original estimates are not exceeded. You may not have the bargaining power of a major insurance company, but you are no less entitled to know what a lawyer proposes to do for you and how much it will cost. It is not enough to simply retain a lawyer and then sit back and wait for wonders to happen. They won't.

You must ask the attorney what he or she thinks about your chances of success and why. You need to find out what the lawyer proposes to do to maximize your chances of success. You need to know whether your attorney believes your expectations are realistic, and if not, why not. If you and your attorney cannot come to terms on this, you may need a different lawyer—one who believes in your cause. You need to know how long your lawyer expects the case to take and why. You need to get a rough estimate of how much the case will cost and what that estimate is based on, because you need to know ahead of time whether you can afford to fight. The litigation decisions you make will be based, at least in part, on cost factors. If you find out ahead of time what you will be up against in terms of fees, you can make your litigation decisions intelligently.

If you have difficulty eliciting an action plan from the attorney you plan to hire, it may be because he or she is one of the passive litigators described in Chapter 4. Generally speaking, there are two litigation styles for divorce lawyers— those who control the case and those who let the case control them. A controlling lawyer will typically be the first one to serve interrogatories (written questions) on the other side and ask to take the depositions (sworn, transcribed interview) of the other side's witnesses. A passive lawyer will typically do nothing until he or she receives interrogatories from the other side, and then all of his or her effort will go into answering them before the time limit expires. Meanwhile, this lawyer will typically have done nothing assertive to make progress on your behalf. Both types of lawyers have plenty of things to do to keep them busy. The difference is that the assertive, controlling lawyer is making things happen, while the passive lawyer is simply reacting to what the controlling lawyer does.

An argument can be made that the passive lawyer is cheaper because he or she does only what is absolutely necessary and doesn't initiate anything. The problem with the passive lawyer is that all he or she does is temporary damage control. Sooner or later, the trial date will be upon you, and if your passive lawyer hasn't done any affirmative preparation, you may lose.

Of course, if both you and your spouse have passive lawyers, having a passive lawyer will not be as big a problem as it would if the other side had a controlling lawyer and you had a passive lawyer. But how will you know ahead of time whether your spouse's lawyer is going to be passive or controlling? Just to be safe, get yourself a controlling lawyer.

How can you determine if a lawyer is passive or assertive? A passive lawyer will have difficulty giving you a detailed, written plan of action for your case. This is because passive lawyers don't know what they are going to do until they see what the other side does. Controlling lawyers, on the other hand, don't really care what the other side is going to do, because they are too busy planning what *they* are going to do. A controlling lawyer has an agenda, and the items on it get accomplished. A passive lawyer waits to find out the other side's agenda items and then either follows along or argues with them. Don't be misled into believing that your lawyer is controlling because he or she constantly refuses to cooperate with the other side's demands. The mark of a controlling lawyer is not refusing to meet the other side's demands; rather, it is making demands of the other side.

Sticking with a Plan

A lawyer may have every intention of being assertive, aggressive, and in control of the litigation and then, for whatever reason, fail to deliver on that promise. Take the case of Jeanette. She wanted an aggressive, spare-no-expense lawyer. She found someone who professed to be unstoppable, who claimed he would represent her as aggressively as anyone possibly could. He mapped out the strategy he planned to follow in her case and showed her the form interrogatories and requests for production of documents he would file together with the complaint for divorce should Jeanette hire him. Jeanette was impressed with the lawyer's enthusiasm and hired him immediately.

Jeanette's attorney filed the initial papers as promised and then started to drift away from her case. The other side had not answered the interrogatories after thirty days, yet her lawyer did nothing. Jeanette wondered what was going on and called her lawyer, who told her he would follow up. He didn't. The next thing Jeanette knew, she was being asked to answer interrogatories from the other side—even though they had never answered hers. She asked her lawyer why this was so, but he simply advised her to get to work answering the questions.

Even though this scenario does not spell disaster, it does portend problems down the road. After a strong start, Jeanette's lawyer started losing steam. This could happen for any number of reasons:

1. He could be too busy with more urgent matters and be putting Jeanette at the bottom of his to-do list.
2. He could be avoiding the case because it is not enjoyable to work on.
3. Jeanette may not be paying her bills on time, so her attorney is working for clients who do pay on time.
4. He could be trying to save Jeanette fees because he is pretty sure the case will settle.
5. He could have every intention of getting back to work on Jeanette's case just as soon as he drums up a few more clients to solidify his cash flow, but right now new client development is taking up most of his time.

Whatever the reason, Jeanette needs to find it out and get to work correcting the problem. She should not stew in silence or hope the problem will go away on its own. The more she allows her case to be ignored, the more it will be ignored. And the sooner she gets rid of an unsatisfactory lawyer, the sooner she can start salvaging her case.

Fortunately, when Jeanette hired her attorney, she insisted that he give her a written action plan listing all the things he planned to do in an effort to win her case, including an estimate of when each task would be accomplished. Without that written plan, Jeanette would have had no clue what was supposed to happen in her case. The plan looked something like this:

ACTION	TARGET COMPLETION DATE
File complaint	February 1
Serve interrogatories and request documents	February 15
Review responses to interrogatories and document production and follow up, if necessary	May 1
Hire expert witnesses	June 1
Move for psychological exam	July 1
Complete interviews of our potential lay witnesses	August 15
Take spouse's deposition	September 1
Depose spouse's witnesses	October 10–15
Trial	January 15

Jeanette set up a meeting with her lawyer and brought the action plan with her. She pointed out that many of the items had not been accomplished by the estimated dates and voiced concern that there might be insufficient time left before her trial to get ready. In this way, she was able to get her attorney to focus on her case. He set up a revised action plan with new deadlines, and this time he completed tasks on schedule. Jeanette's action plan enabled her to track the progress of her case. Without the action plan, she might not have realized that her case was not progressing, and she would not have been able to take steps to get it back on track.

Once you have read and understood the contract (including financial arrangements), made any appropriate changes, and have a written action plan in hand—once all of the things are to your satisfaction—it's time for you and the lawyer to sign on the dotted line. Congratulations—you've hired a divorce lawyer!

6

Communicating with Your Lawyer

Talking with your lawyer is not like talking with your best friend. Although you want to have open and easy communication with your lawyer, you must remember to stay focused on the issues your lawyer wants you to address and not overwhelm him or her with inappropriate demands and superfluous information. For your pocketbook's sake, avoid taking up your lawyer's time in nonproductive ways. Using the guidelines in this chapter, you should be able to use your lawyer's time productively and to your own benefit.

Tell the Whole Truth and Provide Requested Information Promptly

If your lawyer asks you for information, he or she will be stalled until you provide it. Because your lawyer won't ask for information unless he or she needs it, treat any request for information as an urgent matter.

Moreover, tell your attorney the truth and give a complete picture, not an accurate but incomplete one. Don't try to make yourself look better than you are. Your lawyer needs to know the whole truth about you, warts and all. Why? Because it is your lawyer's job to make you look good, and he or she can't do that without knowing about your flaws, shortcomings, and skeletons in the closet.

Suppose you are HIV-positive and have been convicted (albeit many years ago) of child molestation. You fear that you will lose custody of your son if this information becomes known. But if you conceal the information from your attorney, he or she can't develop a plan for dealing with it. Armed with the facts, he or she may decide to retain an expert to testify that your HIV-positive status poses no threat to your child. An expert could also educate the judge regarding your present mental status and whether you are currently at risk for being abusive to your child. Your lawyer might also try to get your case before a judge who tends to ignore child abuse or one who is known not to discriminate on the basis of HIV.

The sooner your lawyer knows of the weaknesses in your case, the sooner he can get started developing a plan to overcome them. If the other side has the information and springs it on your lawyer at trial, your lawyer will appear incompetent to the judge. Remember, your spouse knows a lot about your past and will be feeding all sorts of negative information about you to his or her own lawyer. Don't risk your lawyer's credibility (or your own) by withholding potentially damaging information. Better to get everything out in the open so the damage can be controlled.

Have a Legitimate Reason to Call Your Lawyer

The stress of a divorce and especially the behavior of your spouse can put you on edge. Because financial and child-care arrangements are up in the air, and because spouses can be uncooperative regarding these matters, planning anything is extremely difficult. It's almost as if your life is not your own. If you are lucky enough to have a job, you probably go to work each day wondering how much of the money you are earning will be taken away and given to your spouse and whether you will have any funds left after paying the spouse, the child support, and the lawyers.

It's not surprising then that whenever your spouse acts unexpectedly or something happens that could worsen your plight, you feel like calling your lawyer and passing along the information. Sometimes, though, what has happened does not need to be communicated to your lawyer at all. Other times, the information can be written down and mailed or faxed instead.

Let's say your ex is supposed to bring Bobby back at 7:00 P.M., but he doesn't bring him until 7:30. Let's say this happens at least once a week. Do you need to call your lawyer at 7:30 P.M. each time your ex is late? Unless your lawyer specifically tells you to, don't call. This type of information can certainly wait until normal business hours and can even be communicated in a letter—assuming that a hearing, trial, or other court proceeding is not imminent.

Always pause and reflect before calling your lawyer. Ask yourself: *Do I need to call about this, or would a letter be more effective?* A letter serves the dual function of apprising the lawyer of the information and putting the information in writing. If you tell your lawyer something over the phone, either the lawyer must write it down at your expense or it won't get written down, thereby increasing the likelihood that it will be forgotten.

Before you call your lawyer, ask yourself what you expect the lawyer to do with the information you are sharing. If all you want is for your lawyer to commiserate with you about your misfortunes, consider calling someone else instead—a close friend, a relative, a helpline, a spiritual counselor, or a therapist. By repeatedly calling your lawyer about legally insignificant spousal transgressions, you not only inflate your bill but also run the risk of alienating your lawyer.

Keep a Written Record of Everything

Events will occur that you might think are legally significant but are not. There may also be issues that you consider insignificant on which your lawyer will place great emphasis. In a lawsuit, things that start out as irrelevant details sometimes wind up years later being the crux of the case. The best way to keep track of details—both significant and insignificant—is to keep written records of everything. Keep a journal memorializing each day's events, and let your lawyer know that you are keeping it so he can ask for it if he needs to. Your journal may be used as evidence at trial. Keep it as factual as possible and do not put private thoughts into it.

Keep copies of everything you send your lawyer and everything you get from your lawyer. It is helpful to file the papers in date order so that you can find them when necessary. Never let anyone borrow your only copy of something. The time it takes to make a photocopy is minimal compared with what could occur if an important document were lost.

It is also helpful to keep a log of your oral communications—and attempts at communication—with your attorney. Although I consider myself well organized and focused, I can remember more than one occasion when my lawyer returned a call of mine and I could not remember why I had called in the first place. I usually ended up neglecting to cover some of the subjects I had originally wanted to discuss. Likewise, there will no doubt be times when you call your lawyer about something important, but by the time your call is returned, some other emergency has cropped up and the issue you intended to raise becomes lost in the shuffle. Or what if you place several calls to your lawyer about separate issues, but he or she doesn't call you back until the fourth call? Will you remember what all four of your issues were? What if you feel as if your lawyer never calls you back, but he or she insists that all your calls are in fact returned?

Make a copy of the "Phone Log" in Appendix D and keep it near your phone or with your divorce paperwork. Each time you place a call to your attorney, make the appropriate entries in the phone log: date, time, reason for the call, and what you were told and by whom. For example, if your lawyer was not in when you called, and you were told that he would return your call later that day, write that information down, together with the name of the person you spoke with. That way, when the lawyer does return your call, you can go to your log and remember why you called him. When a call is returned, make the appropriate entries in the last two columns—the date, time, and duration of the return call. By using a phone log, you will be able to keep track of whether your calls are returned, how long calls lasted (to verify the accuracy of your bills), and what each call was about. If your lawyer repeatedly fails to return your calls, the log will serve as documentation when you write to the lawyer or a disciplinary body about the problem.

Keep Your Account Current

Legal representation is not something you are entitled to. It is a service you must pay for, just as you pay for food, clothing, utilities, and car repairs. You would not expect a towing service to tow your car for free if you broke down on the highway but couldn't afford to be towed. Nor should you expect your attorney to represent you for free just because you are in a messy divorce and can't afford to pay.

Don't be lulled into thinking that you can let your unpaid legal bills pile up simply because your lawyer says nothing about them. It could be that your lawyer doesn't have the time or energy to confront you about your bills. Most likely what will happen is that no one will say anything about the unpaid bills, but at the same time your attorney will do lackluster work or put your case on the back burner until you get caught up on your payments. Your attorney may begin to resent you for being so inconsiderate when he or she is putting in so much effort on your behalf. Even though you may not be confronted directly about late payments, the quality of your representation may suffer as a result.

Some attorneys believe that a client who does not have the cash and is not willing to take out a loan to pay the retainer is not worthy of their representation. The rationale for this attitude is this: if you would take out a loan for a car or a house, why not something as important as a divorce? If you consider your divorce or custody fight less significant than a car, some lawyers will perceive you as not being serious enough about the litigation to be a cooperative client.

They will realize that their bills will be at the bottom of your pile.

Attorneys don't want to wait to be paid any more than you want to wait to have your phone calls returned. Your attitude about your legal bills is extremely important. Show that you understand the value of your lawyer's time, and he or she will find it easier to respond to your legal needs.

Be Polite

Common sense tells you to be polite to your lawyer, but as your case goes on, you may find this difficult. Not being a psychologist, I cannot explain why it happens, but divorce lawyers seem to be a natural target for clients' hostility toward their spouses and the judicial system. The longer a case goes on, the more frustration and hostility mount. If your lawyer is the bearer of bad tidings, the temptation is great to lash out at him or her. Resist the temptation. It will have the same effect on your lawyer's attitude toward you as not paying your bill.

Although a good lawyer will be able to help you through minor crises and should be able to let a certain amount of negative emotion roll off his or her back, making a habit of being hostile to your attorney will only undermine your case. Use the same manners with your lawyer that you would like him or her to use with you. Remember, your lawyer is a person with feelings, and if you make his or her life too difficult, you may find yourself shut out of it.

7

Common Client Mistakes

Going through a divorce takes away your security. You are losing a spouse, you may have to move, you may lose custody of your children, and your possessions and money may be taken away. Feeling disoriented and unsure of yourself, you might

- lose your perspective
- be unable to figure out what to do
- believe you deserve what the other side is trying to do to you
- wonder whether the judge will believe what the other side is saying about you
- cry on your lawyer's shoulder
- be paralyzed by threats your spouse is making
- wonder whether you should file bogus criminal charges against your spouse

- think about letting your children know what an awful person their other parent really is
- do nothing because you know once you tell your story to a judge everything will be OK

Although many people have these feelings, letting such thoughts turn into action can lead to serious problems. This chapter examines some of the unpleasant reactions people have to the divorce process and explains how to deal with them in a constructive way.

Having Unclear Objectives

One of the biggest mistakes you can make is to go through the litigation without knowing what you hope to accomplish. If you know what you want to get out of the litigation, you will feel less lost and confused. If you know where you are going and have a plan for getting there, you will be able to assess your progress and make adjustments in your plan if necessary. Without a plan, you will be doing nothing more than paying attorney bills and wondering how long the whole thing can continue. Just as your attorney needs an action plan (see Chapter 5), you need one of your own.

Before you can formulate a list of objectives, you must sift through your personal feelings and those of your spouse to determine what motivates each of you. Try to distinguish what you really want from how you react to your spouse. Also consider why your spouse may be acting a certain way. Because each divorcing spouse experiences the dissolution of a marriage differently, one person is usually in more of a hurry than the other to be divorced, and one person is usually hurting more than the other. If you can identify these different motivations and keep them separated in your mind from the goals you are trying to achieve, you will be less confused as your litigation progresses.

If you have plans to remarry soon but your spouse feels no sense of urgency about the divorce (or wishes to postpone your remarriage), your spouse may use the situation as a negotiating tool and force you to give up a larger share of the assets. If one spouse has more earning potential than the other, the economically dependent spouse may fight the divorce in order to keep his or her hooks in the other's income. An abusive or controlling spouse may resist a divorce or insist on custody of the children as a way of continuing to exert control over the other person. Some people are so fearful of being alone that maintaining a connection, even through something as unpleasant as an ongoing divorce, gives them comfort. Other people view the divorce process as an opportunity to harass and punish their spouse or to drain his or her financial resources.

Negative emotion is to be expected as part of getting divorced. If you face the fact that you are going to have to deal with it, your divorce will proceed more smoothly than if you try to deny it and then lose control when it occurs. Divorcing couples have been irrational and cruel to each other since the beginning of time, and if you manage to escape from a marriage unscathed, consider yourself a member of a very tiny club. Even the ultra-civilized elite of the early 1900s were spiteful in divorce. The following passage from an article in the *Baltimore Sun* (May 16, 1995) about local historical architecture illustrates the extremes some people will go to for revenge.

> In their day, these monolith-like buildings—erected between 1912 and 1926—were a cornerstone of Baltimore social life and housed many prominent city families. One of the most notable was Capt. Isaac Emerson, a lavishly

wealthy man and founder of the drug company that made Bromo Seltzer.

Local lore has it that Captain Emerson built the Emersonian as part of a vicious spat with his ex-wife. Mrs. Emerson lived in a mansion the couple had built at 2500 Eutaw Place, and the Captain supposedly had the Emersonian built to block her view of the lake.

With all the emotional subtext in a divorce, winning means different things to different people. Moreover, even for the same person, what constitutes a win may change over time, depending on that person's emotions and finances. If your spouse has left you for someone else, in the beginning you may feel so angry that nothing short of the death of your spouse would feel like winning to you. But over time, as you get used to the idea that your spouse has left, you may decide that you are happier without him or her. At that point, you may be less interested in paying a divorce lawyer to fight over the dishes and VCR. You might prefer to start afresh with new dishes.

That is why, while it may be tempting to allow your emotions to dictate what you do during your divorce case, this approach can be dangerous. If you don't have a focus—and hence a frame of reference against which to measure your progress—you run the risk of having the litigation get out of control like a runaway truck—with you footing the bill. If you allow your emotions and your reactions to your spouse's legal strategies to control your decision making, you may run out of money before you achieve your desired result. In fact, you may be so busy reacting to your spouse that you don't know what your desired result is!

Once you have separated out your emotional baggage, identify your goals and objectives, and put them in order of importance. Work with your lawyer to determine which issues are urgent and which can be left for later. Your list may look something like this:

- Get spouse out of the house or find new living arrangements for myself.
- Prevent spouse from snatching children.
- Make sure the mortgage gets paid even though spouse has control of all money.
- Protect my business from ruinous claims by spouse.
- Prevent spouse from cleaning out joint accounts and assets.
- Determine what assets I have and which of them are subject to claims of spouse and to what extent.
- Clarify temporary living arrangements for children.
- Deal with harassing phone calls and/or other harassing contact from spouse.
- Decide whether to file for divorce.
- Decide whether to countersue if spouse has already filed.
- Determine whether I want sole custody, joint custody, or no custody of children.
- Determine what my child support obligation will be.
- Determine spouse's position on custody.
- Determine likelihood of success at obtaining custody arrangements I want.
- Determine whether any issues can be settled.
- Determine the mental status of spouse.

It is important that you address living arrangements as soon as possible. If you and your spouse have been living together and the impending divorce means that one of you will have to move, that issue must be addressed right away. If you don't know where you will be living, if you worry every day that when you come home the locks on your house will have been changed, or if your spouse has disappeared with all the money and the bank is foreclosing on your house, you won't be able to function at work or on a personal level.

You must focus on finding a place that can be your sanctuary while the divorce battle plays itself out. Do not overlook the importance of having a place where you can feel safe. Whether that means getting a protective order to keep your spouse away, going to a shelter, moving in with relatives, getting an apartment, or buying a new house, this is the first issue you must resolve. Until you have a home base, you will be useless to yourself and to your children.

If you fear for your physical safety, but your lawyer doesn't seem to be taking you seriously or has been unable to get the court to help (which is often the case), consult with a support group or helpline for battered spouses. Tell anyone who might be able to help about the problem. Keep reaching out for help until you get it. Contrary to what your spouse, or even the judge, might be telling you, being abused by a spouse is *not* your fault. Don't be ashamed to ask for help.

If you have young children, the next issue you must address is where they will live until the court determines custody. Keep in mind that, in a custody battle, you will be judged based on how well you keep the best interests of your children in the forefront. Judges and mental health professionals generally believe that children are best served by having two parents, and that it is not in a child's best interest to have one parent prevent the child from having a relationship with the other parent. If you take the children away from their other parent during the custody fight, your spouse may accuse you of depriving the children of a relationship with him or her. In general, the more flexible and accommodating you are about allowing your spouse to have time with the children, the more kindly the court system will look upon you in the end. However, if you move out of the family home and leave the children with the other parent, this may be construed by the court as an indication that you abandoned the children and do not care about them.

Of course, there are cases where general principles do not apply, and your case may be one. You need to discuss the specific facts of your case with your attorney in order to determine what approach to take. For example, if you must leave town to find work or for some other reason, it may not be possible to devise a schedule where both parents see the children regularly. If your spouse is abusing your child, it may not be appropriate for him or her to be alone with the child. Your lawyer needs to advise you on how to handle such situations.

Once the issues of where you and the children will live are resolved, and when and under what circumstances the children will see their parents, you can begin to address the other issues on your list. Work with your lawyer to prioritize your goals; then write down what has to be done to accomplish each. You will be responsible for some of these things and your lawyer for others. Next to each item, pencil in the date by which you and your lawyer propose to have it accomplished. When your list is complete, you will have your own action plan that you can use to periodically monitor the progress of your case and the effectiveness of your attorney. If at any time your case does not appear to be progressing, take a moment to assess the reason. Perhaps it's your own procrastination, your lawyer's failure to accomplish promised tasks, or new legal issues popping up—any of these things could prevent you from focusing on your intended goals. Take appropriate steps to correct any problems and get back on track.

Your action plan is like a to-do list. Often when we feel overwhelmed by all the work we have to do, when we feel as though—despite working many hours—we are not getting anything done, it is helpful to make a to-do list and then check off items as we accomplish them. This allows us to see written evidence that we have, in fact, accomplished a great deal, even though it may not feel like it.

Succumbing to the Other Side's Mental Engineering

Another common mistake you must not make is to allow the other side's head games to bother you. Before you embark on a divorce or custody fight, even before you go lawyer hunting, take an emotional inventory. Do you feel scared, angry, weak, powerful, afraid, confused? If you feel angry and powerful, that's great. If you feel weak, afraid, or confused, you need to get your thoughts organized and make a plan so you can start to feel less so.

Once the fight begins, not only will you be under siege legally, but you will be under attack mentally and emotionally. Not only will your spouse be your adversary, but he or she will have a powerful ally in the form of an obnoxious, intimidating attorney. You will have to be—and you *can* be—strong enough to withstand this attack.

If you want (and can afford) the help of a therapist, by all means, explore this option, as long as your lawyer has no objections. Align yourself with friends, neighbors, family, support groups, spiritual counselors, parents of your children's friends, and anyone else you can think of. Remember that roughly half of all marriages end in divorce. You are not the only one going through this. There are people out there who have been where you are, or *are* where you are, who can help you. They can say and do things that will help you maintain a positive attitude.

It is up to you to ask for help when you need it and to take care of yourself as the battle rages. Think of yourself as a football player. When a play-off game is approaching, football players eat right and exercise. They eliminate distractions from their lives so they can train for the big game. They analyze the opponent's strengths and weaknesses and plan a strategy accordingly. They don't cower in fear and fantasize about the worst. Rather, they ready themselves for the fight. This is how you should approach your lawsuit. One thing you can do to prepare yourself for the fight ahead is to anticipate the four most common mind-manipulation techniques employed by divorcing spouses:

- Threats and intimidation
- Criminal charges
- Spouse-bashing and brainwashing of children
- Psychologists and other paid experts

Threats and Intimidation

From the very moment you begin to pursue the course of obtaining a divorce or custody, expect threats and intimidation from your spouse and his or her lawyer. They may file pleadings and papers in court demanding that your spouse be given everything—the kids, the cars, the house, child support, alimony, the pension money, the investments, and whatever else there is. Usually such papers demand that, in addition to giving your spouse everything, you should also be required to pay for his or her lawyer.

These tactics are standard operating procedure, and your lawyer should counter by making the same demands of the other side, if he or she hasn't already. Divorce litigation is a two-way street, and you have as good a chance (or better) as your spouse of being awarded these things. If you come from a position of inner strength rather than fear or weakness, if you keep your wits about you and don't give up, you will be able to work things out with your spouse *and* be happy with the result. It may take years, but it is possible.

Threats and intimidation are but one part of the arsenal of tactics you should expect your ex and his or her lawyer to use on you. Discuss each new threat or intimidation tactic with your lawyer and then respond appropriately. If, however, your ex is committing crimes—such as stalking you, attacking you, or harassing you—unless your lawyer has some compelling reason not to, consider reporting the crimes to the police and seeking advice from a local support group. Your lawyer should take your spouse's threats seriously and respond appropriately, but you should not take them personally. Just like the tantrums of a two-year-old, these threats and intimidation tactics can be unpleasant, disruptive, and even dangerous. But as long as you stay cool and display strength and equanimity, the tantrum will eventually end and the child—or your spouse—will be off on another pursuit soon enough.

Even though dealing with the threats and intimidation launched against you by your spouse can be difficult, time-consuming, and financially and emotionally draining, do not let them distract you or your attorney from your own action plan. One of the main reasons for your spouse's attacks is to weaken your resolve to fight for what you want. It is often more effective for you to go on the offensive yourself than it is to get caught up in defending yourself against your spouse's attacks. A good lawyer should be able to manage both offense and defense at the same time.

Criminal Charges

The specter of divorce proceedings will most likely bring out the worst in your spouse, who may even try to commit a crime against you or accuse you of committing one against him or her—or both. My ex and his lawyer used a number of techniques to try to gain advantage during our divorce and custody dispute. For almost two years, I made repeated attempts to gain access to my clothes, furniture, and other items I had left behind in our jointly owned house that he continued to occupy. When I finally went to the house with movers to retrieve some of the items, he retaliated by filing felony theft charges against me. The morning of the trial, the prosecutor dropped the charges, presumably because removing one's own property from one's own house is not a crime. My ex-husband is but one of countless divorcing spouses who could not resist the temptation to involve the criminal justice system in his divorce. If this happens to you, the stakes will immediately go up, as will your legal expenses. Had I been convicted of the charges leveled against me, I could have had my law license revoked and been left without a means of supporting myself and my children.

I thought my case was one of the more extreme ones until I spoke with a stepmother whose husband's ex-wife, in a bid to regain custody of her son, falsely accused the stepmother of sexually abusing the child. The allegation resulted in a nightmarish investigation by child-welfare authorities that eventually vindicated the stepmother and was a death knell to the biological mother's bid for custody. When chil-

dren are involved, some parents feel justified in doing anything and everything not to lose them.

If you are accused of crimes by your ex, you may need
to hire a criminal-defense lawyer, in addition to your divorce
lawyer. Don't take matters into your own hands. Don't lose
hope. Just play by the rules and hang in there. Judges have
very little sympathy for parents who make false allegations
of child abuse. It is such a common tactic in custody battles that, even when a spouse is in fact abusing a child,
courts may refuse to believe it. If your spouse falsely accuses
you of a crime, in most states you can sue him or her in civil
court for damages—attorneys' fees, lost wages, and emotional distress.

Spouse-Bashing and Brainwashing of Children

Even if your spouse's behavior is as offensive as humanly
possible, it would be a mistake to allow your negative feelings toward your spouse to become known to your children
(unless your children are adults). Psychologists believe that
young children identify with both parents and may not be
able to distinguish a verbal attack on a parent from an attack
on themselves. Your children deserve to grow up loving both
of their parents; take that away, and you hurt your children.
If your child has witnessed your spouse physically attack you
(or engage in some other antisocial or pathological behavior) and he or she asks you about it, by all means let your
child know that the behavior is unacceptable and that you
will not tolerate it. If you limit your criticism to the unacceptable behavior and steer away from personal attacks on
the other parent, your child will emerge from the trauma of
divorce with more of his or her self-esteem intact. In addition, you will strengthen your custody case because you will

not be guilty of spouse-bashing. In general, judges tend to frown on parents bad-mouthing each other to the children. Doing so shows bad judgment, a lack of maturity, and poor parenting skill.

If your spouse is physically or sexually abusing your child, however, you *must* discuss this fact with your attorney. There is a possibility that you will be able to find a judge to help you protect your child, but you could wind up in front of a judge who thinks you are making it all up. You must spare no expense to hire the best lawyer available to help protect your child without risking losing him or her.

Sometimes one parent will try to influence a child to prefer him or her over the other parent for purposes of gaining custody. In their book *Children Held Hostage: Dealing with Programmed and Brainwashed Children*, mental health professionals Stanley S. Clawar and Brynne V. Rivlin examine the techniques such parents use. Because the stakes are so high in custody disputes (loss of custody can also mean the loss of one's house, the making of substantial child support payments, and a concomitant diminution in one's lifestyle), parents may consciously or unconsciously try to convince their children that the other parent is unworthy. Clawar and Rivlin describe a number of such techniques, including:

- Attacking or demeaning the other parent
- Pretending the other parent doesn't exist
- Putting the child in the middle between the two parents
- Withholding love unless the child turns against the other parent
- Creating a belief in the child that the other parent's love is not sincere
- Being overindulgent

- Undermining the other parent's authority
- Being the child's "best friend" rather than the traditional authority figure

The authors examine these techniques in detail, describe how children are adversely affected by them, and outline actions the target parent can take to defend against them. The authors stress the importance of providing the child with a positive self-image and observe: "If children adopt a belief that a parent is bad, evil, immoral, inadequate, or deficient as depicted by a programmer who labels him or her as such, the children may come to identify the same negative qualities within themselves."

If brainwashing or programming could be an issue in your custody case, address your concerns with your attorney. It may be appropriate to involve an expert familiar with these issues to advise you and help educate the judge.

Psychologists and Other Paid Experts

Just as there are bad doctors and bad lawyers, there are also bad psychologists and social workers. Just as there are public officials who can be bought, there are also psychologists who can be bought.

Take the case of Miranda. Her former husband was a spouse abuser with a history of mental problems, so when his lawyer, Mr. Crook, wanted a psychologist to do an "independent evaluation" for custody purposes, Miranda was puzzled. Because it seemed so obvious to her that her ex was emotionally unbalanced and violent, she wondered why Mr. Crook would want to draw attention to his own client's mental and behavioral deficits.

Mr. Crook succeeded in getting a court order appointing a psychologist, Dr. Disingenuous, to do an evaluation.

Dr. Disingenuous could require Miranda to come to his office, either alone or with one or both children, as many times as he wanted—and Miranda had to pay him nearly two hundred dollars per hour. Miranda's puzzlement turned to concern when she realized that the doctor's eyes glazed over and he stifled yawns whenever she spoke to him. By the time Dr. Disingenuous was finished with her, Miranda had been given a battery of tests and paid Dr. Disingenuous three thousand dollars!

Miranda felt nausea rising in her throat the afternoon Dr. Disingenuous was to testify when, outside the courtroom she heard Dr. Disingenuous, who would not return *her* lawyer's phone calls, refer to Mr. Crook by his first name. At that moment, Miranda realized that Mr. Crook, Dr. Disingenuous, and her ex-husband were in this together. Imagine her despair when the doctor then proceeded to testify that Miranda's move out of the family home to escape her ex's violent rages was not in the children's best interest. He recommended that the children be moved to a new school of their father's choosing. On the witness stand, Dr. Disingenuous denied knowing about episodes of violence perpetrated on Miranda by her ex-husband—episodes that Miranda had described in a letter to the doctor. Dr. Disingenuous's testimony resulted in Miranda's losing custody of her children.

Miranda was lucky. She was able to afford to pursue this unjust result to a higher level and get it overturned the following year. In the meantime, because of the judge's ruling, Miranda saw her children only a few days per month. The enormous expense of an appeal could have been avoided, and the damage to Miranda's relationship with her children prevented, if only her attorney had hired a psychologist at the beginning to testify on her behalf at the trial. This would have leveled the playing field and defused any advantage Miranda's ex was deriving by using Dr. Disingenuous.

Miranda's case was only one of many in which Dr. Disingenuous and Mr. Crook have been involved. In a significant number of Mr. Crook's cases, either Dr. Disingenuous was appointed by the court to be an "independent" expert or Mr. Crook sent his client and the client's children to Dr. Disingenuous as patients and then used the doctor as an expert at trial. Either way, Dr. Disingenuous consistently opined that Mr. Crook's clients should have custody. No matter whether the client was a spouse abuser, drug abuser, or suicidal manic-depressive, the psychologist always found—or made up—a reason why Mr. Crook's client was the better parent.

Miranda is not the first parent, nor will she be the last, to be victimized by unethical lawyers who refer their clients to unethical psychologists in exchange for favorable courtroom testimony. The legal system encourages this abuse by allowing psychologists to make handsome livings off their courtroom testimony, for which they often charge more than they do to see patients in their offices.

The more a psychologist functions in the domestic-relations litigation milieu, the more relationships he or she develops with lawyers. A divorce lawyer's clients often need therapy, and the more clients a lawyer refers to a given psychologist, the more likely that psychologist will be to remember the source of the referrals when it comes time to testify in court. Dr. Disingenuous no doubt realizes that the referrals from Mr. Crook will dry up pretty quickly if he starts testifying against Mr. Crook's clients in court. To make matters worse, lawyers who develop cozy relationships with psychologists and later become judges often see no reason why they should not continue to favor their friends by appointing them to do "independent evaluations" in divorce cases they are presiding over.

The system provides few, if any, safeguards to prevent unethical divorce lawyers, and even judges, from having dual relationships with these so-called experts. If you are victimized by such conduct, you could file a grievance against the psychologist with your state's licensing board or a psychologists' professional trade association. But proving to a licensing board that a particular psychologist is unethical or has a dual relationship with a lawyer is extremely difficult due to the subjective nature of a psychologist's testimony. If you file a complaint against such a psychologist, you may be perceived as someone with an ax to grind because the psychologist testified against you. Your allegations may not be taken seriously unless you bring in an expert of your own, whom you will have to pay. Is this a detour in your action plan you can afford to make? The best way to protect yourself from such a scheme is to make sure your lawyer knows enough to get you your own expert to cancel out the one on the other side. Unfortunately, experts do not come cheap.

Many lawyers hire expert witnesses as a matter of course when custody is an issue. Other lawyers never even think of it. If you have a contested custody case and your lawyer does not propose retaining an expert, find out why. Urge your lawyer to investigate whether the other side's expert (or the court-appointed expert) gets referrals from or has a history of cases with your ex's lawyer. By ignoring the possibilities, you could end up in Miranda's shoes.

Becoming Discouraged

Now that you have read something about how a divorce progresses, you can probably see the similarities between a divorce and many of life's other challenges: a golf game, an election campaign, repairing a funny noise in the toilet, the quest to get pregnant, a war. First, pick a challenge from your past. Do you remember how things started out and then changed direction and how, as a result, you felt alternating elation and despair? Remember the unpredictable twists and turns you took on your way to the final result? Remember how it took much longer than you had originally thought it should?

As your divorce progresses and your nerves start to fray, compare the divorce to those other struggles. You are going to have ups and downs, but having a bad day does not mean that all is lost. Look at your action plan and see how far you have come. The emergencies that seemed so important last month have faded away, only to have their places taken by new ones. Divorce is a process, and for every problem that crops up, there are several ways to fix it or turn it to your advantage—as long as you persevere. Hang on to your perspective and your sense of humor. If you have children, you need to rise above the mudslinging and get on with living and having a positive relationship with the kids.

Using Your Lawyer as a Therapist

Many times, you will be tempted to talk to your lawyer about your personal problems, particularly since he or she is right in the middle of the action. Resist the temptation. Your lawyer is not trained to help you with nonlegal issues. Although they can and should give you the legal perspective on your problems and help you understand what your rights are and what you risk by making certain choices in the litigation, lawyers cannot help you deal with feelings such as rage and depression. Talk to your lawyer about your feelings only to the extent that the lawyer encourages it, and only for purposes of establishing whether your fears are legitimate and what you can do about them legally.

Once your lawyer gives you the lay of the legal land, if you still cannot cope emotionally, find someone better equipped to help, such as a therapist, rabbi, minister, or priest. Let your lawyer know if you are contemplating counseling. He or she should find out whether what you say to a counselor will remain confidential and immune from being subpoenaed or whether your spouse could get hold of your records and use them against you in the litigation.

In any event, do not bore your lawyer with tirades against your spouse. First of all, you will be charged for the time and will have gotten absolutely nothing for your money. Second, subjecting your lawyer to your negative emotions could make him or her angry or annoyed at you or your spouse, thus making him or her less objective and therefore less effective.

Remember, your lawyer's job, ultimately, is to get the judge to decide your way. If he or she can settle your case before the trial, so much the better. But to do this your lawyer needs to be able to view your case from the judge's perspective—not just yours. Use your lawyer as a weapon in your struggle to win your divorce or custody case, but keep that struggle separate from your other struggle—to heal yourself emotionally.

Expecting to Get Justice by Going to Court

Many people naively believe that, if they can just get the judge to listen to what their ex did, the judge will make things OK. Well, it doesn't work that way. Why not?

In some jurisdictions, judges are appointed as part of a political process and are therefore not answerable to the electorate, other than possibly having to run in infrequent "retention elections." Their biases, values, and belief systems are often more in sync with the political cronies who control the system than the people who appear before them. Even judges who are elected come with no guarantee of open-mindedness. In fact, many judges who routinely hear divorce cases become jaded and callous, adopting the attitude that if two grown people cannot resolve their differences without resorting to the courts, then they deserve whatever result the system decides to impose.

Because there are two sides to every story, judges often find it impossible to figure out who is right or who is telling the truth in the short time they have to deliberate. Instead of trying to figure out the truth themselves, some judges look for a way out. Some will hand the matter off to a social worker or psychologist to "evaluate," often at great expense to the divorcing spouses.

Just as often, a judge will apply direct pressure to the lawyers and litigants to work it out among themselves. Sometimes a judge politely asks the parties involved to work it out themselves. It is not uncommon, though, for divorce judges to lecture, belittle, shame, threaten, and punish litigants in an effort to get them to work it out or to get one party to give in to the other. Some judges are purposely irrational, unpredictable, inconsistent, rude, or insensitive, perhaps in the hope that the parties will be sufficiently cowed to agree on a resolution rather than taking the risk of letting the judge decide for them.

Take the case of Roslyn Smith, reported in the Maryland Special Joint Committee on Gender Bias in the Courts report issued in 1989. Ms. Smith sought help from the court system after her husband threatened to kill her with his gun. She told the committee:

> The thing that has never left my mind from that point to now is what the judge said to me. He took a few minutes and he looked at me and he said, "I don't believe anything that you're saying." He said, "The reason I don't believe it is because I don't believe that anything like this could happen to me. If I was you and someone had threatened me with a gun, there is no way that I would continue to stay with them. There is no way that I could take that kind of abuse from them. Therefore, since I would not let that happen to me, I can't believe that it happened to you."
>
> I have just never forgotten those words. . . . When I left the courtroom that day, I felt very defeated, and very powerless and very hopeless, because not only had I gone through the experience which I found to be overwhelming, very trying and almost cost me my life, but to sit up in court and make myself open up and recount all my feelings and fear and then have it thrown back in my face as being totally untrue just because this big man would not allow anyone to do this to him, placed me in a state of shock which probably hasn't left me yet.

Or take the case of Kathleen Murphy, a bank teller who lost custody of her five-year-old son to her former husband, a lumber company executive. According to newspaper reports, the judge awarded her ex-husband exclusive use of the family house and ordered her to pay him $315 per month in child support, even though at the time she was only earning $7 per hour. Ms. Murphy told the *Baltimore Sun*, "After you put your faith in the judicial system for your whole life and something like this happens to you, you go home and suffer in silence."

Or take the case of Vivian Archie. Although the Tennessee state judge handling her custody case was convicted of sexually assaulting her, his conviction was later overturned. A federal judge who disagreed with this result explained why:

> The theory of the felony counts was that the [state judge] willfully—and repeatedly—used the powers of his judicial office to coerce a woman named Vivian Archie into fellating him on pain of losing her child. Mrs. Archie was physically restrained throughout these assaults, according to her testimony, and she was afraid to scream for help because of the [state judge's] implied threats to deprive her of the custody of her little girl. The jury evidently thought that Mrs. Archie was telling the truth—and if the jury was right in this, it is hard for me to imagine a more clear-cut deprivation of liberty.*

People going through divorce often see their own position as the "right" one and cannot believe a judge won't see it the same way. But a trial is not about the truth; it is the telling of a story. What the judge hears will depend on how good a storyteller your lawyer is and how convincing you and your witnesses are. If you are stiff and wooden or overly emotional and hysterical, the judge may not believe you— or may sympathize with your spouse. The judge may have gone through a messy divorce herself, and you may remind

---

*U.S. v. Lanier, 73 F. 3d 1380 (1996). The U.S. Supreme Court also disagreed with the overturning of the judge's conviction and sent the case back for reconsideration.

her of her ex-husband. The judge could have a very negative reaction to you for some reason, and you may never know why. Although judges are supposed to be trained to put aside personal prejudices and biases, is this really possible? You must realize that whenever you turn a decision over to a judge, as opposed to reaching agreement with your spouse, you are both handing over control to someone else—someone about whom you know very little and over whom you can exert only as much influence as your lawyer can muster.

Your lawyer may try to put certain things into evidence before the judge that are excluded for technical reasons. For example, things other people have told you may be excluded because they are hearsay. Some things may be ruled inadmissible because the judge finds them to be irrelevant. And certain people may not be willing to get up on the witness stand and testify against your spouse under oath because they are afraid of repercussions. What actually comes out at a trial may not bear any resemblance to the way things really are.

Let's suppose, though, that your lawyer does a good job, and all the evidence you wanted to put before the judge for consideration is admitted. You succeed in proving that your spouse, a manic-depressive taking lithium, has a house full of guns and a stockpile of food she plans to eat while living in the underground bomb shelter she insisted on building for use when the roving bands of social misfits take over the country. It may seem crystal clear to you, and everyone you know, that your wife is a nut, but don't be so sure the judge will necessarily come to the same conclusion. You may believe your gun-toting, manic-depressive wife is not a competent parent, but the judge may believe that everyone has a right to bear arms and that, as long as the manic-depressive is taking her medication, she can parent effectively. The judge may view the bomb shelter and food stockpile as legitimate precautions in a world where anything can happen. There are two ways to view every story.

Because judges are so unpredictable, if your legal position is less than clear-cut, it might make sense for you to compromise with your spouse and settle the case. You will not only save on fees but also avoid the risk of getting a bad ruling from the judge.

Even if you win your case and are totally vindicated at the trial level, your spouse can always appeal, thus creating more delay and expense, and possibly win the appeal. For this reason, even if you know you are right, it sometimes makes sense to give up a little and settle, so you can have the fight over sooner, more cheaply, and on terms you can live with.

8

Is Something Wrong Here?

How to Tell When It's Time to Switch Lawyers

It is the rule, not the exception, that things will not go smoothly in a contested divorce case. That doesn't necessarily mean it is your lawyer's fault. And even if it is your lawyer's fault, that doesn't necessarily mean you should fire your lawyer. When you're in the thick of battle and everything seems to be going wrong—the judge is sniping at you, your money is running low, and you haven't seen your children in a month—how do you decide whether to stick with the lawyer you've got or find someone new?

When you feel the need to lash out, and your lawyer is the most convenient target, stop and ask yourself these five questions:

1. Has my lawyer failed to follow the action plan?
2. Has my lawyer lied to me, misused my funds, or falsely billed me?
3. Has my lawyer failed to communicate with me?

4. Has my lawyer been intimidated?
5. Has my lawyer been unprepared or otherwise given up any of my rights without my consent?

If you cannot answer yes to any of these questions, then—objectively speaking—your lawyer is probably doing an acceptable job. Instead of firing your lawyer, wait out the storm and see if things don't improve with time. As in any protracted contest—be it a war, an election, or a board game—both sides in a divorce will have their ups and downs. Switching lawyers for no good reason will not help. It wastes valuable preparation time, and it is expensive.

On the other hand, how do you know if you have a good reason to fire your lawyer? Let's consider each of the five questions.

Has My Lawyer Failed to Follow the Action Plan?

If your lawyer hasn't followed the action plan (discussed in Chapter 5) or some amended version of it, this is a sure sign that the lawyer is not doing a proper job. After all, the action plan is simply the lawyer's own description of how he or she should handle your case. If your lawyer fails to follow this self-written job description, how much worse could things be? As soon as you become aware that your lawyer has missed deadlines or items on the action plan, *you* must spring into action and bring the breach to your lawyer's attention. Do not second-guess yourself; you need not be concerned that you are overreacting or misinterpreting the law. All you are doing is monitoring the action plan that the lawyer devised and pointing out that it is not being followed.

When you point out a breach in the action plan, your lawyer will respond in one of three ways: (1) by correcting the problem and not repeating it, (2) by correcting the problem but still failing to follow the action plan, or (3) by refusing to acknowledge that a problem exists and trying to make you feel in some way mistaken or at fault. The response you want, of course, is the first one. If your lawyer corrects the problem and does not repeat it, then you should feel comfortable continuing with that lawyer. All lawyers get off schedule now and then. As long as no harm has been done to your case (or any harm done has been rectified), then one slip should not be grounds to terminate the representation.

If you receive the second response and the lawyer continues to make promises that are not kept, then you will be caught in a gray area. You will have to weigh the difficulty of overseeing and prodding your present lawyer against the inconvenience and expense (and uncertainty) of hiring a new one.

If you receive the third response—the lawyer refuses to acknowledge the problem or, worse yet, tries to make you feel that it is only a problem because you are making it one—beware. What you have, at its simplest level, is a lawyer who promised to do something and is now denying having made such a promise, a lawyer who may be trying to make you feel guilty for expecting him or her to live up to these promises. Such a lawyer is not trustworthy. The longer you stay with this lawyer, the more your problems will multiply.

Has My Lawyer Lied to Me, Misused My Funds, or Falsely Billed Me?

A lawyer has a professional and ethical obligation, imposed by the profession and by the licensing boards, to be honest with clients. Your lawyer does not have any choice about whether or not to tell you the truth. If your lawyer has lied to you about anything, that is reason enough to fire him or her.

Has your lawyer misused funds or falsely billed you? Lawyers get paid for their time. Your lawyer is the only one who really knows how that time is spent. The temptation to add an extra hour or so to the bill can be great. What if you have a two-hour meeting with your lawyer, but the bill you receive says the meeting was three hours long? What if all your ten-minute phone calls show up on the bill as thirty-minute phone calls? What if you ask your lawyer to do something but a secretary does it and you are billed for the work at the lawyer's hourly rate? What if you paid your lawyer a substantial retainer but he or she cannot (or will not) account for where it went? What if you have questions about your bill that your attorney cannot (or will not) answer to your satisfaction? What if your attorney claims to have spent money on expenses for your case (experts, travel expenses, courier service, long-distance charges, etc.) but cannot document these expenses?

Each of these situations is a warning sign that something could be awry. Although it's possible that you just lost track of time and thought the meetings and phone calls were shorter than they in fact were, it's also possible that your attorney is padding the bill. Although it's possible that the fees and expenses are correctly billed, and the lawyer is just too disorganized to be able to reconstruct an itemization, it's also possible that the time and expense charges are fabricated.

A lawyer's client is absolutely entitled to a detailed accounting of all of the time and expense charges billed to him or her. If you suspect a problem, you should write your lawyer a letter and insist on an explanation. If you are not satisfied with the explanation, or if your lawyer ignores your letter, you should seriously consider finding another attorney. If you get a satisfactory explanation and elect to continue using your attorney, use a photocopy of the "Phone Log" (Appendix D) to keep track of the time you spend on the phone or in conference with him or her. Make a note of the time at the beginning and end of each meeting or phone call, and when the bill comes compare your log with the description on the bill. If you are still being overbilled, your completed phone log will document the discrepancies, and you will be able to fire the lawyer without hesitation.

Has My Lawyer Failed to Communicate with Me?

Bestselling books tell us that men and women have vastly different communication styles, so it should come as no surprise that communication between lawyers and clients can also be very difficult. A lawyer might feel as if she has been on the phone all day explaining things to her client, while the client is feeling completely confused and up in the air. Who's to say whether the lawyer has failed to communicate? How does one judge whether the lawyer's communication skills are inadequate or whether the subject matter being communicated is just not comprehensible to the client? How do you know whether switching lawyers would help matters or whether you just don't understand how the system works and never will?

In general, a client is entitled to know what the lawyer recommends and why, how goals will be accomplished, what the other side is doing, what the court is doing, and what any court-appointed specialists are doing—and also to receive an analysis of the significance of these various activities. This type of information should be communicated from the lawyer to the client on an ongoing basis, preferably *in writing*. It is often difficult for a divorce client to listen to a lawyer's spoken words and understand them immediately after a court hearing or other stressful event. A client needs to have information in written form so it can be reread later. Clients also need information in writing so that the course of the litigation can be documented in case any questions arise later about what was recommended, what was done, and why. If you have to switch lawyers, you will save a great deal of time and money if the new lawyer can read the old lawyer's status reports to get up to speed.

Many divorce lawyers do not send clients written status reports. They simply file in court whatever papers they deem necessary or react to the other side's actions and then apprise the client over the phone. This haphazard style results in two problems. First, the lawyer never has to focus on the reasons for his or her actions and whether such actions are advancing the client's interests. Second, the client never gets a chance to read about and reflect on what is happening in the case. The best way to figure out if your lawyer is communicating is to read the status reports. If there are none, ask for them. If, after asking, there still are none, consider looking elsewhere for counsel.

Another communication problem can arise when the client cannot get the lawyer to listen. If your lawyer cannot return your phone call the same day, someone from the lawyer's office should let you know when your call will be returned. It is unacceptable for a lawyer to be inaccessible by phone to clients. Unfortunately, many divorce clients simply cannot reach their lawyers on the phone when they need them. If you have this problem, refer to the guidelines in Chapter 6 about how to communicate with your lawyer. If, after following these guidelines, you find that your lawyer remains virtually incommunicado, don't blame yourself. Look elsewhere for representation.

Has My Lawyer Been Intimidated?

Many victories claimed in divorce litigation occur simply because the other side became scared or gave in. Parents who should be awarded custody give it up rather than go through a mudslinging trial—all because the other lawyer cowed them, and their own lawyer didn't give them enough confidence to carry on. If your lawyer doesn't have enough self-confidence to try your case, how will you? If your lawyer is afraid of the hot-tempered judge, how can you not be? It is a rare lawyer who will ever *admit* having been intimidated, but the fact remains that many lawyers *are* regularly intimidated, both by judges and by opposing lawyers.

Sometimes lawyers avoid making courtroom objections out of fear of annoying the judge. As discussed in Chapter 2, objections are necessary in the event the client should lose and an appeal must be filed. If your lawyer hasn't made the proper objections, it may not be possible for you to appeal because the record will not have been preserved.

Lawyers sometimes give up an argument or a position because the lawyer on the other side has intimidated them— for example, by threatening to file a motion for sanctions. It is improper for lawyers to allow themselves to be influenced by unfounded threats and bully tactics. If another lawyer is bullying your lawyer, think long and hard about keeping that lawyer. You need a lawyer that the other side wouldn't even consider bullying. Like children on a playground, lawyers have an ability to identify and take advantage of the insecure or frightened opponent. If your lawyer has not proved to the opposition lawyer that he or she is bully-proof, let that lawyer represent someone else. You need a more seasoned attorney.

Has My Lawyer Been Unprepared or Otherwise Given Up Any of My Rights Without My Consent?

Sometimes it will be obvious if a lawyer is unprepared; for example:

- The lawyer who comes to court and cannot remember what your case is about
- The lawyer who forgets to show up for a meeting or court hearing
- The lawyer who does not file documents within the appropriate time deadlines
- The lawyer who doesn't devise a plan for your case and then follow through on it
- The lawyer who doesn't meet with you to get information about your case and then interview witnesses
- The lawyer who doesn't research the legal issues
- The lawyer who doesn't consider exploring settlement or alternative dispute mechanisms
- The lawyer who doesn't locate and hire the necessary and appropriate experts

Any of these unprepared lawyers could be forfeiting some of your rights.

A lawyer's lack of preparation can manifest itself in more subtle ways as well. In states that require one to prove certain grounds for divorce, a mutually agreed-upon separation is usually an easier ground to prove than adultery. Yet in these states it may take longer to get a divorce based on voluntary separation than it does to get a divorce based on adultery. Which grounds to allege should be a decision that is ultimately made by the client after listening to the lawyer's recommendation.

Your lawyer should not make strategy decisions without your authorization. Your lawyer should not choose the slow, cheap route over the fast, expensive route without first consulting you. Your lawyer should not unilaterally decide not to pursue certain rights or remedies you may be entitled to without first getting your permission. For example, your lawyer should not give away your chance at a portion of your spouse's pension in exchange for custody of the children *unless you authorize it.* (You may have been able to get both.) A lawyer who preempts your right to choose or exercises it without consulting with you has exceeded the scope of his or her authority and has failed to prepare all aspects of your case properly.

You may be wondering how you would ever find out that your lawyer had given up your rights without your knowledge. It is usually very difficult to find out, especially if you are not an attorney. As my own divorce case was unfolding, I sometimes discussed my attorneys' actions with lawyer friends, one of whom commented that my divorce was not unlike a brain surgeon having brain surgery—except that I was awake throughout the whole ordeal. As unpleasant as it was being awake for the experience, I was able to recognize problems and protect myself.

If you are not a lawyer, you can still protect yourself by assertively monitoring the case, insisting on status reports, and making it your business to understand what your attorney is doing and why. Keep going back to the action plan, month after month, and ask your lawyer how he or she is progressing toward the plan's stated goals. By being visible and assertive and having an ongoing dialogue with your lawyer, you improve your chances of hearing more about your options as the case progresses. You also increase the likelihood that your file will be worked on, as opposed to sitting in the file cabinet waiting for your spouse's lawyer to make a move.

What makes a lawyer well prepared is, in part, that lawyer's level of thoughtfulness and foresight. The ability to map out a strategy for attaining a goal—and then attaining it—will necessarily involve having Plan B and Plan C in mind just in case Plan A does not work. As an active participant in your own case, you will begin to develop a sense for whether your lawyer has a game plan or is just reacting to what is happening around him or her.

You do not need a law degree to spot problems in your case. If something seems questionable, ask your lawyer about it; you are entitled to an explanation. Sometimes the client, who has more knowledge of the facts of the case, will spot issues the lawyer hasn't realized the importance of—or hasn't even noticed.

Over time, you will develop a relationship with your attorney that primarily involves exchanging information. If you are not comfortable with the relationship—if too much information is going from you to the lawyer but nothing is coming back, if it is impossible to give information because the lawyer is inaccessible, if you don't understand what the lawyer is telling you, if the lawyer is telling you things that don't match up with reality—then your lawyer is, in effect, giving up your rights. If you are in the dark, or if your lawyer is in the dark, who is protecting your rights? It may very well be the time to look for a new lawyer.

9

Getting Back on Track

If you find that you have chosen the wrong lawyer, getting back on track requires finding a new lawyer, firing your old lawyer, getting your file to your new lawyer, settling up your account with your old lawyer, and perhaps even suing your old lawyer or reporting him or her to the appropriate authorities.

Finding a New Attorney

Once you have decided to fire your lawyer, the first step is to find a new one. *Do not fire your lawyer until you have hired a new one.* Firing your lawyer in the middle of a divorce or custody case without having a replacement lined up would be worse than taking a quarterback out of the football game without having a substitute available. You already know how important your choice of lawyer can be. Rather than rush into things, simply shop quietly for a new lawyer while keeping your old one. Then, when you hire the new lawyer, have him or her enter an appearance in your case at the same time the old one strikes his or her appearance. In some states, even if you have not paid your bill, a lawyer will not be able to get out of your case without your permission without first obtaining the permission of the court. Under no circumstances should you willingly let one lawyer withdraw from your court case unless you have another one involved. If you let your old lawyer out of the case (or if the court lets him or her out) before you have a new lawyer, your spouse's lawyer will pounce on you so fast your head will spin. You probably won't even know you've been pounced on until it's too late.

When you go looking for a new lawyer, you may find that some won't talk to you until you've fired your old lawyer and settled your bill. Don't waste any time on these lawyers. The only reason they want you to have fired and paid your other lawyer is that they are lazy. They don't want to get in the middle of a dispute between you and your first lawyer. A dispute could arise, for example, if you hire the new lawyer but the old lawyer won't hand over your file until you pay the bill. Suppose you can't pay the old lawyer's bill because you had to pay the new lawyer's retainer? If you've already hired the new lawyer, he or she has a duty to represent you. This is very difficult to do without the file, but the old lawyer is holding it hostage. It's a messy situation, but if the new lawyer is not up to the challenge of getting the file from the old lawyer, you won't be missing out on much by not hiring him or her.

Firing the Old Attorney

Once you have hired a new attorney and that attorney has entered an appearance in your case, discharge the old one. Do this in writing so that you have a record of when you told the attorney to stop working. You don't need a lawyer racking up billable hours after you have fired him or her. Check the terms of your fee agreement to see if there is something special you need to do to fire the lawyer, such as notifying him or her by certified mail.

If the fee agreement states that you cannot fire the lawyer or if the fee agreement has any other provision that you consider onerous or unfair, discuss this either with your new attorney or with the appropriate grievance commission or licensing board in your jurisdiction. Such provisions may not be enforceable.

Getting Your File to the New Attorney

Get your file from the old attorney and take it to the new one. If the split with your old lawyer is amicable, your old lawyer may even offer to send the file to your new lawyer directly. If the split isn't amicable and you owe the old lawyer money, he or she may refuse to give up your file. This may or may not be legal, depending on your jurisdiction, but if you followed the recommendations in Chapters 6 and 8 about getting everything in writing, your old lawyer refusing to give you your file may not be a problem. If you have maintained copies of all the pleadings, status reports, and correspondence, you can simply copy your own file and give that to your new lawyer. He or she can fill in any missing court filings by getting them from the court file or from your spouse's lawyer.

Settling Accounts with the Old Attorney

If you fired your old lawyer for cause, you may wonder whether you should pay your outstanding bill. Because this lawyer has caused you to have to switch lawyers, you have had to hire someone new and pay him or her to read your file and get caught up on your case. This extra expense would not have been necessary if it weren't for the improper behavior of your old lawyer.

Consider asking your old lawyer to reduce his or her bill to counterbalance the expense of bringing in someone new. He or she may be happy to see you go and agree to waive all or part of your bill. On the other hand, the lawyer may pursue you for the unpaid fees. If the lawyer is not too aggressive, you may be able to simply ignore the bills until they stop coming. At the other end of the spectrum, if the lawyer is very aggressive and sues you, your best defense may be to countersue for malpractice.

It is important to keep your main goal in focus at all times. Don't allow a side battle with an unethical lawyer to take your attention from where it should be—namely, on finding a good lawyer and getting your divorce and custody situation resolved.

Suing or Reporting the Old Attorney

If you suspect you may have been the victim of attorney malpractice, ask yourself these questions:

1. Did the lawyer have a duty to do something for me that he or she failed to do?
2. Did that breach of duty cause me damage?
3. How much was the damage?

Lawyers are duty-bound to do certain things for their clients. For example, they can't settle a client's case without the client's permission. When a settlement proposal is made, they have a duty to let the client know about it. They cannot falsely bill. They have to zealously advocate their client's interests. They must answer all legal pleadings within the time provided by the rules unless they have a legitimate extension of time. There are many, many more duties that lawyers have to their clients. If you feel that your lawyer somehow did you a disservice, it is very likely that disservice constitutes a breach of a duty the lawyer owed you.

The hard part is determining whether that breach of duty caused you damage. Suppose the lawyer never sent you copies of any of the pleadings and never updated you on what was happening in your case. He or she breached the duty to keep you informed. But did this breach of duty hurt you in any way? Let's suppose the lawyer forgot to tell you to come to court for the trial, so the trial happened without you even there. Let's suppose the judge divided the money between you and your spouse fifty-fifty but gave no reason for this distribution. Can you win a malpractice case against your lawyer? Only if you can prove that if your lawyer had told you about the trial you would have come to it and that if you had been at the trial, you would have gotten a better result.

In a malpractice case, not only must you prove that your lawyer made a mistake, but you must also prove that it was that mistake that caused you damage. Not that it *might* have caused you damage but that it *more probably than not* caused you damage.

If your attorney did breach a duty to you that caused damage, can you put a dollar figure on that damage? This is not difficult if the damage consists of overbilling or stealing your retainer funds. But if the damage is speculative or remote, or too mixed in with other issues in the case, you may not be able to prove your case with enough certainty.

If you believe you need to sue a lawyer, first think through the issues outlined above, and then try to place the case in the hands of a competent professional-negligence lawyer as soon as possible. The law imposes certain limits on the time you have to sue, known as statutes of limitation and statutes of repose. These vary from state to state and are different for different types of lawsuits. To avoid missing one of these deadlines, you should not delay in consulting a malpractice lawyer. Then, once the case is in the hands of counsel, try to forget about it until the divorce and custody issues are resolved.

Suppose you were the victim of a very poor lawyer but can't answer yes to any of the questions on page 140. Or suppose you simply don't have the stomach for more lawsuits. Is there anything else you can do to prevent this lawyer from victimizing others? Fortunately there is. Check with your state bar association (listed in the "Other Resources" section at the back of this book) to obtain the name, address, and phone number of the appropriate board or commission with which to file a grievance about the lawyer. Attorneys are usually policed by a state agency or self-policed by a board, committee, commission, or similar group. Whatever the oversight entity, it will have a complaint procedure you can follow to make your concerns known. Do not delay in contacting the entity, however, because your right to file a complaint may also be lost with the passage of time.

10

Conclusion

By now you understand how the family-law system functions and what you need to do to find a lawyer who can represent you well in it. As you experience the highs and lows of your divorce with your carefully chosen lawyer by your side, focus on keeping your perspective. Individual events such as losing a discovery motion or saying something stupid in your deposition will probably not make or break your case. Nor does a slam-dunk victory on temporary child support mean you can't lose custody later.

Because obtaining a divorce is a process that takes time and patience to endure, you will fare best if you don't allow the litigation to consume you. Make a special effort to take care of yourself. Spend time with your children and supportive friends and relatives. Pursue your work and hobbies to the extent you can. Keeping yourself busy with things other than the divorce and custody fight and surrounding yourself with supportive people will help you through the litigation. More important, doing these things will make it easier to let go of your spouse and enter a new phase of your life, one that can be as fulfilling as you choose to make it.

Appendix A

Information from Family Members, Friends, and Acquaintances

Lawyer Name _____

Source of Information _____

Date _____

1. Did the lawyer return your phone calls promptly? _____

_____

2. Did the lawyer answer your questions? _____

3. Did the lawyer explain how the process worked and lay out for you the possible results and consequences that could result as you went through each step of the process? _____

_____

_____

_____

4. How much did the lawyer charge? Did the lawyer estimate for you the amount of money the entire process would wind up costing over the long haul? _____

_____

_____

_____

5. How did you feel about the amount you were charged and why?

_____

_____

_____

6. During actual court hearings, depositions, and meetings, did your lawyer make you feel safe and protected? _____

_____

_____

_____

7. Did your lawyer ever treat you as a nonentity? Did you ever feel your best interests as the client were secondary to your lawyer's need to fit in with the lawyers' clique? _____

_____

_____

_____

8. Was your lawyer eloquent? Was your lawyer able to think on his or her feet? _____

_____

_____

9. Did your lawyer remember things you told him or her, or did you find it necessary to provide the same information over and over again? _____

_____

_____

_____

10. Was your lawyer aggressive enough? _____

_____

_____

11. Was your lawyer well prepared and well organized? _____

_____

_____

_____

12. Did your lawyer get ready for important matters such as hearings, depositions, and trials ahead of time, or were these things left until the last minute and then accomplished in a crisis environment?

_____

_____

_____

_____

13. Were your schedule and calendar of commitments taken into account when matters were scheduled, or were you simply told when and where to appear? _____

_____

_____

_____

14. Did you feel your lawyer respected you? If not, why? _____

_____

_____

_____

15. Did you feel your lawyer cared about your situation? If not, why?

_____

_____

_____

16. Was your lawyer organized? _____

_____

_____

_____

17. Did your lawyer have too many other matters going on to pay proper attention to your case? _____

_____

_____

_____

18. Did you ever suspect that the lawyer had a drug or alcohol problem or suffered from a mental disorder or condition (such as Alzheimer's disease)? If so, why? _____

_____

_____

_____

19. Overall, were you satisfied with the communication between you and your lawyer over the course of the case? _____

_____

_____

_____

20. Would you use this lawyer again? If not, why? _____

_____

_____

_____

_____

21. How did your lawyer stack up against your ex's lawyer?

_____

_____

_____

_____

22. Did you fire this lawyer? If so, why? _____

_____

_____

_____

_____

23. Who was your ex's lawyer and what did you think of him or her?

_____

_____

_____

_____

Appendix B

Lawyer Information Summary Sheet

Name _____

Date Interviewed _____

Address _____

Sex _____

Age _____

Phone

    Home _____

    Work _____

    Fax _____

    Mobile _____

Law School Attended _____

Year Graduated from Law School _____

Year Admitted to Practice Law _____

Billing Rate _____

Retainer Required _____

Describe physical appearance of lawyer and his or her office

_____

_____

Eye contact: good _____ poor _____

Attitude: brusque/compassionate/distracted/other _____

_____

_____

Did lawyer genuinely listen to you? _____

_____

_____

_____

Did lawyer allow telephone or staff interruptions? _____

_____

_____

Legal advice: gave none _____ gave helpful advice _____

Energy level: high/medium/low _____

Most memorable quality _____

_____

_____

Most bothersome quality _____

_____

_____

Your feelings after interview _____

_____

_____

Appendix C
Questions for the Lawyer

Name _____

Date Interviewed _____

How long have you been practicing law? _____

_____

How much of your practice is in the field of domestic relations?

_____

_____

_____

Other than domestic relations, what kinds of cases do you handle?

_____

_____

_____

How long have you been doing domestic-relations work? _____

_____

_____

_____

Are you certified as a specialist in domestic relations? ⎯⎯⎯⎯⎯

⎯⎯⎯⎯⎯⎯⎯⎯⎯⎯⎯⎯⎯⎯⎯⎯⎯⎯⎯⎯⎯⎯⎯⎯⎯⎯⎯⎯⎯⎯⎯⎯

⎯⎯⎯⎯⎯⎯⎯⎯⎯⎯⎯⎯⎯⎯⎯⎯⎯⎯⎯⎯⎯⎯⎯⎯⎯⎯⎯⎯⎯⎯⎯⎯

⎯⎯⎯⎯⎯⎯⎯⎯⎯⎯⎯⎯⎯⎯⎯⎯⎯⎯⎯⎯⎯⎯⎯⎯⎯⎯⎯⎯⎯⎯⎯⎯

Who else, other than you, would be working on my case and why?

⎯⎯⎯⎯⎯⎯⎯⎯⎯⎯⎯⎯⎯⎯⎯⎯⎯⎯⎯⎯⎯⎯⎯⎯⎯⎯⎯⎯⎯⎯⎯⎯

⎯⎯⎯⎯⎯⎯⎯⎯⎯⎯⎯⎯⎯⎯⎯⎯⎯⎯⎯⎯⎯⎯⎯⎯⎯⎯⎯⎯⎯⎯⎯⎯

⎯⎯⎯⎯⎯⎯⎯⎯⎯⎯⎯⎯⎯⎯⎯⎯⎯⎯⎯⎯⎯⎯⎯⎯⎯⎯⎯⎯⎯⎯⎯⎯

Tell me about three of your cases that were the most meaningful for you and why. ⎯⎯⎯⎯⎯⎯⎯⎯⎯⎯⎯⎯⎯⎯⎯⎯⎯⎯⎯⎯⎯

⎯⎯⎯⎯⎯⎯⎯⎯⎯⎯⎯⎯⎯⎯⎯⎯⎯⎯⎯⎯⎯⎯⎯⎯⎯⎯⎯⎯⎯⎯⎯⎯

⎯⎯⎯⎯⎯⎯⎯⎯⎯⎯⎯⎯⎯⎯⎯⎯⎯⎯⎯⎯⎯⎯⎯⎯⎯⎯⎯⎯⎯⎯⎯⎯

⎯⎯⎯⎯⎯⎯⎯⎯⎯⎯⎯⎯⎯⎯⎯⎯⎯⎯⎯⎯⎯⎯⎯⎯⎯⎯⎯⎯⎯⎯⎯⎯

⎯⎯⎯⎯⎯⎯⎯⎯⎯⎯⎯⎯⎯⎯⎯⎯⎯⎯⎯⎯⎯⎯⎯⎯⎯⎯⎯⎯⎯⎯⎯⎯

⎯⎯⎯⎯⎯⎯⎯⎯⎯⎯⎯⎯⎯⎯⎯⎯⎯⎯⎯⎯⎯⎯⎯⎯⎯⎯⎯⎯⎯⎯⎯⎯

How do you think the local judges perceive you, and which judge do you think is the best to have in a domestic case? ⎯⎯⎯⎯⎯⎯⎯

⎯⎯⎯⎯⎯⎯⎯⎯⎯⎯⎯⎯⎯⎯⎯⎯⎯⎯⎯⎯⎯⎯⎯⎯⎯⎯⎯⎯⎯⎯⎯⎯

⎯⎯⎯⎯⎯⎯⎯⎯⎯⎯⎯⎯⎯⎯⎯⎯⎯⎯⎯⎯⎯⎯⎯⎯⎯⎯⎯⎯⎯⎯⎯⎯

⎯⎯⎯⎯⎯⎯⎯⎯⎯⎯⎯⎯⎯⎯⎯⎯⎯⎯⎯⎯⎯⎯⎯⎯⎯⎯⎯⎯⎯⎯⎯⎯

⎯⎯⎯⎯⎯⎯⎯⎯⎯⎯⎯⎯⎯⎯⎯⎯⎯⎯⎯⎯⎯⎯⎯⎯⎯⎯⎯⎯⎯⎯⎯⎯

⎯⎯⎯⎯⎯⎯⎯⎯⎯⎯⎯⎯⎯⎯⎯⎯⎯⎯⎯⎯⎯⎯⎯⎯⎯⎯⎯⎯⎯⎯⎯⎯

How do you think the other local domestic-relations lawyers perceive you? _____

_____

_____

_____

_____

_____

How often are you in court? _____

_____

_____

How often are you in court on a domestic-relations matter?

_____

_____

When was the last divorce or custody trial you had? _____

_____

_____

How long did it take? _____

_____

_____

Who was the judge? _____

_____

_____

How many open divorce and custody cases do you have right now?

_____

_____

How many divorce or custody trials have you had in the past year?

_____

_____

Is there a reason there are so many [or so few]? _____

_____

_____

_____

Do you represent both men and women? Why or why not?

_____

_____

Do you feel the system works properly to give fair results? If not, what can you do to increase the chances that I will be treated fairly by the system? _____

_____

_____

_____

How often do you handle appeals on behalf of your domestic-relations clients? _____

_____

_____

_____

How many appeals have you handled in your career? _____

_____

_____

How much do you charge? _____

_____

Do you require an advance retainer, and if so, how much is it?

_____

What do you do with the advance retainer? Is a portion of it reserved
for the final bill? _____

_____

How often do you bill? _____

_____

May I see a sample bill showing what information will be on my bills
and the level of detail? _____

_____

How long after I am billed before payment is due? _____

_____

Do you take charge cards or offer a payment plan? _____

_____

What happens if I cannot pay a bill? Do you immediately terminate
my representation? _____

_____

_____

How much do you estimate my case will cost altogether?

_____

_____

What are the terms of the fee agreement?   _____

_____

_____

How long will it be before the case reaches completion?

_____

_____

_____

Do you require anything from me in the way of information or otherwise before you can decide whether you can undertake my representation, and if so, what?   _____

_____

_____

_____

_____

Have you written any articles or books, given any speeches, or taught any classes on domestic-relations law? If yes, give details and provide copies of the articles.   _____

_____

_____

_____

_____

What is your rating in *Martindale-Hubbell*? _____

What are your activities in bar association groups pertaining to domestic-relations law? _____

_____

_____

_____

_____

Are you involved in any social causes pertaining to domestic relations (e.g., father's rights, domestic violence issues, lobbying or supporting changes in the law as it pertains to divorce and custody)?

_____

_____

_____

_____

_____

What kind of result do you think we should be looking for in my case, and is this a reasonable goal? Do you feel I have any unrealistic expectations? If so, what are they and why? _____

_____

_____

_____

_____

_____

_____

How many cases have you had with my spouse's lawyer, and what are your impressions of that lawyer? _____

_____

_____

_____

_____

If you are not available to take my call, do you have someone else who will be able to speak with me? If not, how long will it take you to return my call? _____

_____

_____

_____

_____

Will you need to hire an expert witness for my case? What will be the areas of expertise and who will you use? How much will this cost?

_____

_____

_____

_____

What are the different phases of my case? Describe briefly how the process will work. _____

_____

_____

_____

My spouse is (or I am) prone to fits of rage and violence. Will this be a factor in my case? _____

_____

_____

_____

_____

Why do you handle divorce cases? Aren't they difficult because of all the negative emotion? _____

_____

_____

_____

_____

Have you ever been suspended, disbarred, or reprimanded? If yes, give details. _____

_____

_____

_____

_____

Have you ever been sexually or romantically involved with one of your divorce clients? _____

_____

_____

_____

This whole process of getting a divorce and having to testify in court has me really jumpy and nervous. I feel like everything is out of control. Is this normal? What should I do? ————————————

————————————————————————————————

————————————————————————————————

————————————————————————————————

————————————————————————————————

Is there anything I haven't asked about that you want to tell me?

————————————————————————————————

————————————————————————————————

————————————————————————————————

Please give me some references (current or former clients).

————————————————————————————————

————————————————————————————————

————————————————————————————————

————————————————————————————————

————————————————————————————————

————————————————————————————————

————————————————————————————————

————————————————————————————————

————————————————————————————————

————————————————————————————————

Appendix D

Phone Log

Date	Time	Reason for Call	To Whom I Spoke	What I Was Told	Duration of Call	Date/Time Call Was Returned

Appendix E
Sample Fee Agreement

LAW FIRM
123 Main Street
Anywhere, USA 00000

Dear Client:

You have asked our firm to act as your attorneys. This letter sets forth the agreement concerning our representation of you. This agreement shall become effective upon our receipt of a countersigned copy of this letter and the retainer fee.

1. We have agreed to represent you and you have agreed to pay us a retainer fee of $5,000.00, a check for which we have already received. Our hourly time charges will be deducted from this retainer. Unless it has been previously expended by virtue of the periodic time billings, the retainer will be credited against the overall fee in your matter when a final billing takes place. Any time previously devoted to your case (including consultation time either unbilled or unpaid) and for which payment has not been made will be charged against the retainer.

2. The final billing is based on hourly charges. It is possible that more than one lawyer in our office will work on your case, since it has been our experience that a

sharing of responsibility within the firm provides better and more efficient representation for the client. Hourly rates for the lawyers who might work on your file range from $75 to $250. We may also utilize paralegal and law clerk support staff whose hourly rates are significantly lower. I will have the primary responsibility for the handling of this matter, and my services will be billed at the rate of $200 per hour. We make every attempt to minimize multiple billing, but there are occasions when it is, in our judgment, necessary for more than one lawyer to work on the file at the same time. This most frequently occurs during conferences concerning the status and planning with respect to your case, in preparation for oral argument of the appeal, and also in the event any hearings are required during trial preparation and during trial. Infrequently, hourly rates change. In the event of an hourly rate change during our representation of you, you will be notified in advance and the revised hourly rate shall become the hourly rate that you will be charged. Obviously, if this change is unacceptable to you, you may notify me and terminate the representation.

3. It is impossible to determine in advance the amount of time that will be needed to complete your case. It is also impossible to project what result will be accomplished. Any and all activities conducted by us will be billed at the aforementioned rate, including the making and receipt of telephone calls; drafting and review of correspondence; preparation and review of court papers and Agreements; research; preparation for oral argument and/or trial; travel time; conferences with you, witnesses, or your former spouse's attorney; participation at oral argument and/or trial, including the time spent awaiting the case to

be called on the date of hearing, etc. The minimum time charge for any activity other than an uncompleted telephone call is 2/10 of an hour.

4. We will bill you periodically on a time-expended basis, at which time charges will be credited against the retainer until it is exhausted. It is your obligation to keep your account current and make payment within ten days of billing. You should review your periodic bill upon receipt and contact us both by phone and in writing with any questions or comments you have. If we do not hear from you to the contrary within ten days of billing, the billing will be deemed to be accurate. We reserve the right to terminate our attorney-client relationship for nonpayment of fees or nonpayment of reimbursable expenses described in the following paragraph.

5. In addition to the above, we will advise you of any monies expended by us on your behalf, such as filing fees, transcripts, and printing costs, for which we will be entitled to reimbursement from you as billed on a periodic basis. The retainer fee is not credited toward disbursements.

6. We will keep you well informed as to the progress of your case. We will send you copies of all papers coming in and going out of our offices, including correspondence, pleadings, and other court documents. The file and its progress are open to your inspection at any reasonable time.

7. Every effort will be made to expedite your case efficiently according to the highest legal and ethical standards.

8. In the event of the termination of our representation, for any reason, prior to substantially concluding your matter, you will be charged for all time expended and all necessary disbursements in connection with the termination prior to the refund to you of the unused portion of the retainer.

9. Please countersign this agreement, so that we will have a mutual memorandum of our understanding, and return your signed copy to us. Upon our receipt of the signed retainer agreement, we will deposit the retainer fee check you provided to us last week.

10. If at any time you have questions concerning our fee arrangement and billing procedures, please feel free to call or write us.

Sincerely yours,

Your New Lawyer

Appendix F

Sample Interrogatories

The following Interrogatories are propounded pursuant to Maryland Rules of Procedure, Rule 2-421, and are to be answered fully and under oath or the grounds for refusal to answer any Interrogatory shall be stated in full. Rule 2-421(b).

(a) These Interrogatories are continuing in character, so as to require you to file supplementary answers if you obtain further or different information before trial.

(b) Where the name or identity of a person is requested, please state full name, home address, and also business address, if known.

(c) Unless otherwise indicated, these Interrogatories refer to the time, place, and circumstances of the occurrence mentioned or complained of in the pleadings.

(d) Where knowledge or information in possession of a party is requested, such request includes knowledge of the party's agents, representatives, and, unless privileged, his attorneys. When answer is made by a corporate defendant, state the name, address, and title of the person supplying the information and making the affidavit and the source of his information.

(e) The pronoun "you" refers to the party to whom these Interrogatories are addressed and the persons mentioned in the clause (d).

1. State your full name, actual home address at which you are residing, business or employment address, condition of your health, date of birth, and social security number.

2. State whether or not you are presently employed (even if your employer is a closely held corporation owned by you), and, if your answer is in the affirmative, state the following for each employment (whether full or part-time): the exact name and address of your present employer; the nature and duties of your present employment and your title, if any; your gross regular weekly, biweekly, semimonthly, or monthly wages or salary, including commissions, specifying the method of payment; your net weekly, biweekly, semimonthly, or monthly wages or salary, including commissions, specifying the nature and exact amount of each and every deduction made by your employer from your gross regular wages; the number of hours of your regular workweek; and the exact number of hours of overtime for which you were compensated in the past twelve months and the gross and net amounts of compensation you received for working that overtime for said period.

3. If you have, during the present year or the past three years received any fringe benefits from any business entity of any nature whatsoever, itemize each fringe benefit received during the last three calendar years on a year by year basis and the present year to date, specifying in your Answer the exact date to which the figure runs; and, if any fringe benefit was paid in money or credited in cash terms, state the amount attributed to each fringe benefit, and, if not paid in money or credited in cash terms, state the monetary value of each fringe benefit, it being understood that this, as well as the other Interrogatories are continuing and require supplementation from time to time to the date of trial.

4. Itemize the sources and amounts of your "gross income," as defined by Section 61 of the Internal Revenue Code for the years 1989, 1990, 1991, and, when available, 1992, specifying in your Answer to this Interrogatory the date to which said figures run, the total allowable tax deductions for each year, and the adjusted gross income you reported to the income authorities for each year, it being understood that this, as well as other Interrogatories propounded, are continuing and require supplementation from time to time to date of trial.

5. Itemize the source and amounts of any other monies or credits received by you during the years 1989, 1990, 1991, and, when available, 1992 not reflected in your Answer to Interrogatory No. 4 including, but not limited to, gifts made to you, loans made to you, loans repaid to you, sale of assets, untaxed distributions from any business or nonbusiness sources, unemployment or disability benefits, etc., it being understood that this, as well as the other Interrogatories propounded, are continuing and require supplementation from time to time to date of trial.

6. If self-employed or a member of a partnership or corporation, state the name under which you, the partnerships, or corporation trades; the type of business of each and every branch office, warehouse, and storage or other operating facility maintained by you or the business entity; and the address of each business. Itemize the income and expenses and assets on a year-by-year basis for the last three calendar years and through the present year to date.

7. If you are a member of a partnership, a principal in a corporation, or an owner or co-owner of any business entity, give the names and addresses of all other partners and/or principals, the business accountant, and the location and custodian of the business records.

8. List each and every parcel of real property, fee simple, or leasehold in the State of Maryland, or elsewhere, in which you individually, or as a member of a partnership or principal in a corporation, or as a co-owner with any other person have any interest whatsoever, giving an accurate location of the property, including street or road address and post office box and route number, if any; the interest held by you and the names and addresses and relationship to you, if any, of all and any co-owners and interest held by each of them; the reference to the deed or other instrument under which you acquired title to the interest held; and the names and addresses of all mortgagees and other persons, natural or corporate, possessing any mortgage lien or other encumbrance upon all or any property or properties listed in answer hereto, stating fully as to each the type of mortgage lien or other encumbrance, the date incurred and/ or acquired, the face amount thereof and balance due thereon as of the date of these answers, the date(s) additional payments are due, and whether or not payments are in arrears.

9. If any of the property or properties listed in Interrogatory No. 8 produce any income, state the type of income produced, i.e., rents, etc.; the amount of income produced and the date and method of payment; and names and addresses of all tenants, renters, and/or others from whom said income is received.

10. Give a complete list of all persons, natural or corporate, who owe you, or any one or more of the partnerships of which you are a member, or a corporation in which you are a principal, any money or accounts receivable and/or who are holding any money or credits to which you, or any one or more of the partnerships of which you are a member, or a corporation in which you are a principal, are or will

in the future become entitled, giving names and addresses, amounts owed or held, and date payable, and state whether you consider same to be collectible or uncollectible.

11. Give a complete list of any and all persons, natural or corporate, whom you, or any one or more of the partnerships of which you are a member, or a corporation of which you are a principal, have contracted to construct any building of any type or to sell any parcel of land which you or such partnership or partnerships now own or have under contract.

12. On each of the transactions listed in answer to Interrogatory No. 11, give the date of contract and type of work to be done or a description of the parcel of land to be sold; amount of contract and date and amount of deposit or down payment; and dates and amounts of all subsequent payments made or to be made in the future; and state balance due to you or the partnership or corporation.

13. List all bank or building and loan or savings and loan association accounts, special, savings, and/or checking, which you now have or have had within the last three years either individually or as a member of a partnership or together with some other persons, natural or corporate, giving the name, address, and occupation of each person, firm, or corporation besides yourself having an interest in the account and the relationship, if any, of each such person to you; date account was opened; present balance; and date account closed, if closed.

14. List all property with a value in excess of $50.00 of every kind, character, and description located in this State or elsewhere in which either you, your spouse, or both of you have any present interest of any nature whatsoever, regardless of how such property is titled or how it was acquired. Such property shall include, but is not limited to, improved

or unimproved real property; condominiums; stocks, bonds (including U.S. savings bonds), debentures, options, and all other securities; bank accounts, including savings accounts, checking accounts, and certificates of deposit; cash; automobiles, trucks, trailers, and vans; boats; home furnishings and appliances; art objects; antiques; collections of any type having any value, e.g., stamp, coin, doll, book, gun, etc.; debts owed to you, your spouse, or you both, whether secured or unsecured; business interests, whether said interest is in a sole proprietorship, partnership, joint venture, or corporation; profit sharing plans; military retirement or disability benefits; pension or retirement rights, whether vested or nonvested or matured or non-matured; life insurance policies; federal or state disability benefits; annuities; worker's compensation claims; claims against another arising from contract or tort; silverware; china; furnishings; jewelry; furs; livestock; farm or gardening equipment; interest in an estate or trust; tax shelters; etc.

15. With respect to each item of property listed in your previous Answer, state how it is titled, its market value, the amount of any present encumbrance thereon or outstanding indebtedness directly traceable to its acquisition (whether or not said indebtedness constitutes an encumbrance thereon), and the name and address of any entity to whom said indebtedness is owed.

16. If you contend that any of the items listed in your Answer to Interrogatory No. 14 are not "marital property," as defined by Md. Code, Family Law Article, Section 8-201(e), identify each item contended not to be marital property, and, as to each, state the facts upon which your contention is based in full. If you have refused to answer the foregoing interrogatory as framed, then as to any item of property referred to in your Answer to Interrogatory No. 15,

state which item or items of property, if any, were acquired by either you, your spouse, or both of you, prior to your marriage to one another, or by inheritance or gift from a third party, or which are excluded by valid agreement from being marital property, or are property whose acquisition is directly traceable to any of those forementioned sources, and for each specific item of property itemized, state the date of its acquisition and the manner or method of its acquisition, e.g., gift from a third party, inheritance, purchase, etc., and if its acquisition is directly traceable to non-marital sources, state that source.

17. If you contend that there are any other assets that meet the definition of "marital property," as set forth in Md. Code, Family Law Article, Section 8-201(e), which assets have not been referred to in your Answer to Interrogatory No. 15, itemize that property and state the approximate value of each item listed. If you have refused to answer the foregoing Interrogatory as framed, then list all property not itemized in your answer to Interrogatory No.14 with a value in excess of $50.00 located in this State or elsewhere in which either you, your spouse, or both of you have any present interest of any nature whatsoever, and which property was acquired by either you, your spouse, or both of you during your marriage to one another, excluding, however, all property acquired prior to your marriage to your spouse, all property acquired by inheritance or gift from a third party and all property excluded by valid agreement from being marital property, and all property directly traceable to those forementioned sources, and state the value of each item of property listed and date and method or manner of its acquisition.

18. Submit a current, detailed, and itemized statement of your present assets and liabilities, stating the now value

of each asset and, if any other person or entity has an interest in said asset, the name of the person who has said interest and that person's percentage share of ownership.

19. State whether during the period between January 1, 1989, to date you have owned or had an interest in any life insurance or annuity policy, and, if so, for each policy state the name and address of each insurance company; the number of the policy; the type of policy; the date the policy was issued; the face amount of the policy; the amount of the annual premium; the total amount of premiums paid on the policy; the name and address of each beneficiary named in the policy; the date of any change of beneficiary and the name of each beneficiary added or deleted during the period between January 1, 1989, and the present; the date of assignment of the policy and the name of each assignee, if the policy has been assigned; the name and address of the insurance agent or broker for the policy; the amount, date, and present balance of each loan made on the policy, if any; and the present cash surrender value of the policy.

20. If you have any interest in any type of retirement, profit sharing, deferred compensation, or pension plan or fund, including an Individual Retirement Account or Keogh Plan, state: the name of the plan or fund; the name and address of the custodian or administrator of the plan or fund; the percent of your present vesting in the plan or fund; the name of any employer contributing to the plan or fund, if any; the total amount of your contributions to the plan or fund; the total amount of your employer's contributions in your behalf in the plan or fund, if determinable; the present balance of your interest in the plan or fund, if determinable; the earliest date upon which you are entitled to receive actual benefits from the plan or fund; the amount of benefits and the method of payment to you on

retirement of any funds from said plan or fund; the amount of any funds now available to you and the method of obtaining them; whether you have in your possession the plan or fund document and any amendments thereto or, if not, a written summary of the plan or fund and, if not, the name and address of the person from whom they may be obtained; the date to which your last annual plan or fund benefit statement runs; the usual date upon which the annual plan or fund benefit statement is issued; your beginning date of employment with the originator of the plan or fund; the date upon which you began participation in the plan or fund; your last date of employment with the originator of the plan or fund, if your participation has been terminated; the present value of your interest in the plan or fund; and itemize your last five years of compensation on a year-by-year basis for plan or fund purposes, if relevant to plan participation.

21. Are you the legatee, devisee, or beneficiary of any will, estate, or trust fund; and if so, give the nature of the interest, the amount payable and when it is or will be received, and reference to any court proceedings.

22. Are you the plaintiff or judgment creditor in any cause of action; if so, give the title of said cause of action and the name of the court in which same is filed.

23. Is there any pending litigation (including worker's compensation) to which you are a party, in any Court or administrative agency; or is there any action in which you claim or anticipate any settlement or monetary recovery?

24. State the name and address of any expert whom you propose to call as a witness in this proceeding and specify the field of his expertise and attach to your Answers a copy of any written reports or the summary of any oral reports furnished to you by any such expert.

25. During your marriage to your spouse and since the time of your separation from your spouse, have there been any bank accounts, on which your name did not appear, in which you deposited money; and if so, for each account state the name and address of the bank, the name under which the account stood, the account number, and the approximate date and amount of each deposit made by you.

26. If you contend that your spouse is not a proper person to have the care and custody of your minor children, state the facts upon which such contention is based and give the names and addresses of all persons having knowledge of such facts.

27. Describe in detail your present child-care plan (the child-care plan which you would be prepared to offer if the child was in your custody) and state the name of all persons caring for the children, the hours during which you would utilize their services, and whether they would care for your children in your home or elsewhere.

28. State whether you have sought or received treatment of any kind or nature, including, but not limited to, therapy, psychiatric treatment, or treatment for alcoholism or drug abuse, at any time during the past three years.

29. Itemize all expenses paid by you for the benefit of any children of the parties, including, but not limited to, medical, dental, and educational expenses.

30. State the name and address of any person not above mentioned who has personal knowledge of facts material to this case, and the name and address of any and all individuals you intend to call as witnesses in the trial of this matter.

Appendix G
Sample Bill

LAW FIRM
123 MAIN STREET
ANYWHERE, USA 00000

AS OF 1/31/95   LAST DATE BILLED THRU 0/00/00
95004-JOE CLIENT
001-RE DOMESTIC

JOE CLIENT
789 BLANK AVENUE
ANYWHERE, USA 00000

PROFESSIONAL SERVICES

DATE		HOURS
BY: LAWYER #1		
1/13/95	CONFERENCE WITH CLIENT	1.00
1/22/95	REVIEW OF MOTION AND MEMO	.50
1/23/95	REVIEW OF PROPOSED	
	MOTION AND CORRESP	.50
TOTAL:	2.00 HOUR AT 275.00 PER HOUR	$550.00
BY: LAWYER #2		
1/13/95	REVIEW OF DOCUMENTS	1.00
1/16/95	REVIEW OF FILE	
1/16/95	ORGANIZATION OF DOCUMENTS	
1/16/95	REVIEW OF LETTER FROM CLIENT	2.50
1/17/95	REVIEW OF FILE	
1/17/95	DRAFT MOTION	3.50

1/18/95	RESEARCH	
1/18/95	DRAFT MOTION	
1/18/95	ORGANIZATION OF DOCUMENTS	6.00
1/19/95	RESEARCH	
1/19/95	DRAFT MOTION	
1/19/95	REVIEW AND REVISE MOTION	
1/19/95	REVIEW OF LETTER FROM CLIENT	
1/19/95	REVIEW OF CORRESPONDENCE	
1/19/95	FILE WORK	6.00
1/20/95	REVIEW AND REVISE MOTION	
1/20/95	TELEPHONE TO COURT	
1/20/95	FILE WORK	1.00
1/23/95	LETTER TO CLIENT	
1/23/95	TELEPHONE FROM CLIENT	
1/23/95	FILE WORK	.70
1/25/95	ORGANIZATION OF EXHIBITS	
1/25/95	TELECONFERENCE WITH CLIENT	
1/25/95	ORGANIZATION OF DOCUMENTS FOR FILING	
1/25/95	TELEPHONE TO CLERK OF THE COURT	
1/25/95	LETTER TO CLERK OF THE COURT	
1/25/95	LETTER TO CLIENT	
1/25/95	FILE WORK	2.30
1/26/95	LETTER TO OPPOSING LAWYER	
1/26/95	FILE WORK	
1/26/95	TELEPHONE TO CLIENT	.50
1/27/95	TELEPHONE FROM OPPOSING LAWYER	
1/27/95	MEMO TO FILE	
1/27/95	FILE WORK	.60
1/31/95	TELEPHONE TO CLIENT	
1/31/95	FILE WORK	.20

TOTAL: 24.30 HOUR AT 215.00 PER HOUR $5,224.50

BY: LAWYER #3

1/13/95	MEETING WITH CLIENT	.85
1/30/95	FILE WORK	.75
TOTAL:	1.60 HOUR AT 180.00 HOUR	$288.00

BY: LAW CLERK

1/23/95	GET COPY OF CSA OPINION/LETTER	1.75
	TO CT CLR	
TOTAL:	1.75 HOUR AT 75.00 PER HOUR	$131.25

BY: PARALEGAL

1/31/95	OBTAIN COPY OF DOCKET SHEET	.20
	FROM COURT	
TOTAL:	.20 HOUR AT 80.00 PER HOUR	$16.00

CURRENT SERVICES RENDERED $6,209.75

DISBURSEMENTS

DUPLICATING
TOTAL FOR MONTH OF 1/95	$183.80
TOTAL TYPE	$183.80

FILING & MISC. FEES
TOTAL FOR MONTH OF 1/95	$60.00
TOTAL TYPE	$60.00

MISCELLANEOUS
TOTAL FOR MONTH OF 1/95	$7.09
TOTAL TYPE	$7.09

CURRENT DISBURSEMENTS $250.89
RETAINER CREDIT
TOTAL CURRENTLY DUE $6,460.64
PREVIOUS ACCOUNTS RECEIVABLE BALANCE
PAYMENTS THIS MONTH

TOTAL BALANCE DUE $6,460.64

Appendix H

Sample Letters

Return My Call

789 Blank Avenue
Anywhere, USA 00000

Date

Via facsimile and U.S. first-class mail

Lawyer #1
Law Firm
123 Main Street
Anywhere, USA 00000

Re: *Roe v. Doe* (your case name)

Dear Attorney:

I called your office asking to speak with you on May 1, 4, and 8 and have been told each time that you were in trial.

When you finish your trial, or at some other convenient time, I would like to speak with you briefly about your assessment of the progress to date on this matter and your recommendation for how to proceed. Would you please give me a call when you are available to talk?

Very truly yours,

Joe Client

Send Me Copies of Correspondence and Pleadings

789 Blank Avenue
Anywhere, USA 00000

Date

Via facsimile 555-0000

Lawyer #1
Law Firm
123 Main Street
Anywhere, USA 00000

Re: *Roe v. Doe* (your case name)

Dear Attorney:

I recently received from you a copy of a letter you wrote on June 1, 1994, to my spouse's lawyer responding to his letter of May 20. I do not have a copy of the May 20 letter.

Please send me a copy of this letter.

If there is any other correspondence and/or pleadings in this case that you have either received or sent out that you have not sent me copies of, please forward me copies.

Very truly yours,

Joe Client

Send Me a Status Report

789 Blank Avenue
Anywhere, USA 00000

Date

Via facsimile and U.S. first-class mail

Lawyer #1
Law Firm
123 Main Street
Anywhere, USA 00000

Re: *Roe v. Doe* (your case name)

Dear Attorney:

This is in follow-up to our conversation last Wednesday. Would you please let me know what the outcome was of your discussions:

1) with opposing counsel regarding the cancellation of the hearing scheduled for the end of the month, the scheduling of discovery depositions of the parties, and the production of documents; and

2) with the psychologist regarding the time frame for the rendering of her opinion in written form.

When you have a moment, I would appreciate a status report.

Very truly yours,

Joe Client

Send Me a Copy of a Deposition Transcript

789 Blank Avenue
Anywhere, USA 00000

Date

Via facsimile and U.S. first-class mail

Lawyer #1
Law Firm
123 Main Street
Anywhere, USA 00000

Re: *Roe v. Doe* (your case name)

Dear Attorney:

Did the deposition of the psychologist scheduled for 10 A.M. today occur? If so, would you please send me a copy of the transcript as soon as it becomes available?

Very truly yours,

Joe Client

Questions About My Bill

789 Blank Avenue
Anywhere, USA 00000

Date

Via facsimile and U.S. first-class mail

Lawyer #1
Law Firm
123 Main Street
Anywhere, USA 00000

Re: *Roe v. Doe* (your case name)

Dear Attorney:

I am in receipt of your bill dated July 8. This bill contains an entry on 6/17/96 for one hour to "set up arrangements for visitation the weekend of 6/18 through 6/21."

As far as I know, you did nothing to address the issue. When I tried to reach you to resolve the problem on 6/17, I learned you were out of town through 6/21. Due to your unavailability, I had to muddle through alone. I do not think I should be charged for this time since you did not solve the problem and were out of town.

Also on the bill is a charge of $100.00 for "Filing fee re Rule to Show Cause regarding modification of visitation." Why was this motion filed as a show cause order when an ordinary motion would have been free? I do not believe I should be charged for this unnecessary and unauthorized expense.

I would appreciate your considering these points and making appropriate adjustments to the bill or contacting me to discuss them. Thank you for your consideration in this matter.

Very truly yours,

Joe Client

Here Is Something You Should Know

789 Blank Avenue
Anywhere, USA 00000

Date

Via facsimile and U.S. first-class mail

Lawyer #1
Law Firm
123 Main Street
Anywhere, USA 00000

Re: *Roe v. Doe* (your case name)

Dear Attorney:

Enclosed is a copy of the letter I received from my spouse yesterday that you and I discussed in our phone conversation of this morning.

Very truly yours,

Joe Client

Other Resources

Books

The American Bar Association Guide to Family Law: The Complete and Easy Guide to the Laws of Marriage, Parenthood, Separation, and Divorce. American Bar Association (Chicago), 1996, 170 pages, $12.00

American Bar Association Publications
750 North Lake Shore Drive
Chicago, IL 60611
(800) 285-2221

Children Held Hostage: Dealing with Programmed and Brainwashed Children. Stanley S. Clawar, Ph.D., C.C.S., and Brynne V. Rivlin, M.S.S. American Bar Association (Chicago), Section of Family Law, 1991, 197 pages, $49.95

Divorced from Justice: The Abuse of Women and Children by Divorce Lawyers and Judges. Karen Winner. HarperCollins Publishers (New York), 1996, 329 pages, $24.00.
E-mail: kwinner@divorcedfromjustice.com

Win Your Child Custody War. C. Hardwick. Pale Horse Publishing, 1995, 550 pages, $87.55
P.O. Box 2569
Omalaska, TX 77360
(800) 646-5590
E-mail: palehors@indirect.com

Organizations

Fathers United for Equal Rights
P.O. Box 511
Randallstown, MD 21133
(410) 764-9340

Mothers Without Custody
P.O. Box 36
Woodstock IL 60098
Enclose self-addressed business-size envelope with 64¢ postage.

National Coalition for Family Justice, Inc.
821 Broadway
Irvington-on-Hudson, NY 10533
(914) 591-5753

Websites

http://www.divorceinfo.com

http://www.divorce-online.com

http://www.indirect.com/www/palehors

http://www.divorcedfromjustice.com

Bar Associations

American Academy of Matrimonial Lawyers
150 North Michigan Avenue, Suite 2040
Chicago, IL 60601
(312) 263-6477
fax (312) 263-7682

American Bar Association
Family Law Section
750 North Lake Shore Drive
Chicago, IL 60611
(312) 988-5613
fax (312) 988-6800

Alabama State Bar
Family Law Section
415 Dexter Avenue
P.O. Box 671
Montgomery, AL 36101
(334) 269-1515
fax (334) 261-6310
E-mail: info@alabar.org

Alaska Bar Association
Family Law Section
P.O. Box 100279
Anchorage, AK 99510-0279
(907) 272-7469
fax (907) 272-2932

State Bar of Arizona
Family Law Section
111 West Monroe Street, Suite 1800
Phoenix, AZ 85003
(602) 252-4804
fax (602) 271-4930

Arkansas Bar Association
Family Law Section
400 West Markham Street
Little Rock, AR 72201-1408
(501) 375-4606
fax (501) 375-4901

The State Bar of California
Family Law Section
555 Franklin Street
San Francisco, CA 94102-8228
(415) 561-8200
fax (415) 561-8228
URL: http://www.calbar.org

The Colorado Bar Association
Family Law Section
1900 Grant Street, Suite 950
Denver, CO 80203-4309
(303) 860-1115
fax (303) 894-0821
E-mail: cobar@USA.net

Connecticut Bar Association
Family Law Section
101 Corporate Place
Rocky Hill, CT 06067-1814
(860) 721-0024
fax (860) 257-4125
URL: http://www.ctbar.org

Delaware State Bar Association
Family Law Section
1201 Orange Street, 11th Floor
Wilmington, DE 19801
(302) 658-5279
fax (302) 658-5212

Bar Association of District of Columbia
Family Law Section
1819 H Street, N.W., 12th Floor
Washington, DC 20006
(202) 223-6600
fax (202) 293-3388
E-mail: barassndc@aol.com

The Florida Bar
Family Law Section
650 Apalachee Parkway
Tallahassee, FL 32399-2300
(904) 561-5600
fax (904) 561-5827
URL: http://ww3.pwr.com/LEGAL/FLABAR/toc.html
E-mail: flabarwm@flabar.org

The State Bar of Georgia
Family Law Section
800 The Hurt Building
50 Hurt Plaza
Atlanta, GA 30303
(404) 527-8700
fax (404) 527-8717

Hawaii State Bar Association
Family Law Section
Penthouse 1
1136 Union Mall
Honolulu, HI 96813
(808) 537-1868
fax (808) 521-7936
URL: http://www.hsba.org

Idaho State Bar
Family Law Section
525 West Jefferson Street
P.O. Box 895
Boise, ID 83701
(208) 334-4500
fax (208) 334-4515

Illinois State Bar Association
Family Law Section
424 South Second Street
Springfield, IL 62701
(217) 525-1760
fax (217) 525-0712

Indiana State Bar Association
Family Law Section
230 East Ohio Street, 4th Floor
Indianapolis, IN 46204-2199
(317) 639-5465
fax (317) 266-2588
E-mail: isbaadmin@inbar.org

The Iowa State Bar Association
Family Law Section
521 East Locust Street
Des Moines, IA 50309
(515) 243-3179
fax (515) 243-2511

Kansas Bar Association
Family Law Section
1200 Harrison Street
P.O. Box 1037
Topeka, KS 66601-1037
(913) 234-5696
fax (913) 234-3813
E-mail: ksbar@ink.org

Kentucky Bar Association
Family Law Section
514 West Main Street
Frankfort, KY 40601-1883
(502) 564-3795
fax (502) 564-3225
E-mail: postmaster@kybar.org

Louisiana State Bar Association
Family Law Section
601 St. Charles Avenue
New Orleans, LA 70130
(504) 566-1600
fax (504) 566-0930

Maine State Bar Association
Family Law Section
124 State Street
P.O. Box 788
Augusta, ME 04332-0788
(207) 622-7523
fax (207) 623-0083
E-mail: info@mainebar.org

Maryland State Bar Association
Family Law Section
520 West Fayette Street
Baltimore, MD 21201-1767
(410) 685-7878
fax (410) 837-0518
E-mail: msba@msba.org

Massachusetts Bar Association
Family Law Section
20 West Street
Boston, MA 02111
(617) 338-0500
fax (617) 542-3057

State Bar of Michigan
Family Law Section
306 Townsend Street
Lansing, MI 48933
(517) 346-6300
fax (517) 482-6248
E-mail: webmeister@michbar.org

Minnesota State Bar Association
Family Law Section
514 Nicollet Mall, Suite 300
Minneapolis, MN 55402
(612) 333-1183
fax (612) 333-4927

The Mississippi Bar
Family Law Section
643 North State Street
P.O. Box 2168
Jackson, MS 39225
(601) 948-4471
fax (601) 355-8635
E-mail: msbar@mslawyer.com

The Missouri Bar
Family Law Section
326 Monroe Street
P.O. Box 119
Jefferson City, MO 65102
(573) 635-4128
fax (573) 635-2811
E-mail: mobar@mobar.org

State Bar of Montana
Child and Family Law Section
46 North Last Chance Gulch, Suite 2A
P.O. Box 577
Helena, MT 59624
(406) 442-7660
fax (406) 442-7763

Nebraska State Bar Association
Family Law Section
635 South 14th Street, 2nd Floor
P.O. Box 81809
Lincoln, NE 68501
(402) 475-7091
fax (402) 475-7098
E-mail: nsbasn01@nol.org

State Bar of Nevada
Family Law Section
201 Las Vegas Boulevard S., Suite 200
Las Vegas, NV 89101
(702) 382-2200
fax (702) 385-2878

New Hampshire Bar Association
Family Law Section
112 Pleasant Street
Concord, NH 03301
(603) 224-6942
fax (603) 224-2910

New Jersey State Bar Association
Family Law Section
New Jersey Law Center
One Constitution Square
New Brunswick, NJ 08901
(908) 249-5000
fax (908) 249-2815

State Bar of New Mexico
Family Law Section
5121 Masthead Street N.E.
P.O. Box 25883
Albuquerque, NM 87125
(505) 797-6000 or (800) 876-6227
fax (505) 828-3765

New York State Bar Association
Family Law Section
One Elk Street
Albany, NY 12207
(518) 463-3200
fax (518) 487-5517

North Carolina Bar Association
Family Law Section
8000 Weston Parkway
Cary, NC 27519
(919) 677-0561
fax (919) 677-0761

State Bar Association of North Dakota
Family Law Section
515½ East Broadway, Suite 101
P.O. Box 2136
Bismarck, ND 58502-2136
(701) 255-1404
fax (701) 224-1621

Ohio State Bar Association
Family Law Section
1700 Lake Shore Drive
P.O. Box 16562
Columbus, OH 43216-6562
(614) 487-2050
fax (614) 487-1008

Oklahoma Bar Association
Family Law Section
1901 North Lincoln Boulevard
P.O. Box 53036
Oklahoma City, OK 73152-3036
(405) 524-2365
fax (405) 524-1115

Oregon State Bar
Family Law Section
5200 S.W. Meadows Road
P.O. Box 1689
Lake Oswego, OR 97035
(503) 620-0222
fax (503) 684-1366
E-mail: postmaster@asbar.org

Pennsylvania Bar Association
Family Law Section
100 South Street
P.O. Box 186
Harrisburg, PA 17108-0186
(717) 238-6715
fax (717) 238-1204

Rhode Island Bar Association
Family Court Bench Bar Committee
115 Cedar Street
Providence, RI 02903
(401) 421-5740
fax (401) 421-2703

South Carolina Bar
Family Law Section
950 Taylor Street
P.O. Box 608
Columbia, SC 29202-0608
(803) 799-6653
fax (803) 799-4118

State Bar of South Dakota
Family Law Committee
222 E. Capitol Avenue
Pierre, SD 57501-2596
(605) 224-7554
fax (605) 224-0282
E-mail: tbarnett@sdbar.org

Tennessee Bar Association
Family Law Section
3622 W. End Avenue
Nashville, TN 37205
(615) 383-7421
fax (615) 297-8058
E-mail: prestba@aol.com

State Bar of Texas
Family Law Section
1414 Colorado Street
P.O. Box 12487
Austin, TX 78711-2487
(512) 463-1463
fax (512) 463-1475

Utah State Bar
Family Law Section
Utah Law and Justice Center
645 S. 200 E., Suite 310
Salt Lake City, UT 84111
(801) 531-9077
fax (801) 531-0660

Vermont Bar Association
Family Law Committee
P.O. Box 100
Montpelier, VT 05601
(802) 223-2020
fax (802) 223-1573
E-mail: bpaolini@vtbar.org

Virginia State Bar
Family Law Section
707 E. Main Street, Suite 1500
Richmond, VA 23219
(804) 775-0500
fax (804) 775-0501
URL: http://www.vsb.org

Washington State Bar Association
Family Law Section
2101 Fourth Avenue, 4th Floor
Seattle, WA 98121-2330
(206) 727-8200
fax (206) 727-8320
E-mail: barchief1@adl.com

West Virginia State Bar
Family Law Committee
2006 Kanawha Boulevard, E.
Charleston, WV 25311
(304) 558-2456
fax (304) 558-2467

State Bar of Wisconsin
Family Law Section
402 W. Wilson Street
P.O. Box 7158
Madison, WI 53707-7158
(608) 257-3838
fax (608) 257-5502
URL: http://wisbar.org

Wyoming State Bar
Family Law Section
500 Randall Avenue
P.O. Box 109
Cheyenne, WY 82003
(307) 632-9061
fax (307) 632-3737

Glossary of Legal Terms

action   Lawsuit.

agreement   Facts and issues the parties do not dispute, often reduced to writing in the form of fee agreements, separation agreements, and settlement agreements.

allegation   Claim or contention made during the course of the lawsuit.

annulment   The dissolution of a marriage, because it was not valid to begin with.

appeal   The process of trying to undo or reverse a court's decision.

appellant   The person filing an appeal.

appellate court   The court in which an appeal is pursued.

bar association   Association of lawyers grouped by geographic location or subject matter of practice.

brief   A document submitted to the court explaining one side's position.

case   The elements one side needs to prove at trial to win; or, more generally, a lawsuit.

caseload   All the cases being handled by a particular lawyer, law firm, or judge.

child support   Money paid by one parent to the other to cover some or all of the costs of caring for their child or children.

closing argument The lawyer's final remarks made to the judge at the conclusion of the trial, summarizing his or her client's position.

conflict of interest A situation in which a lawyer, judge, or witness might not be fair and impartial. For example, a lawyer would have a conflict of interest in representing the wife in a contested divorce if the lawyer or another member of his firm was already representing the husband.

contested divorce A divorce in which the spouses disagree on issues such as whether to be divorced, how to divide assets, alimony, custody, and/or child support.

contingent fee An arrangement in which the attorney does not get paid unless the client wins. This type of arrangement is generally not permitted in divorce and custody cases.

court order A decision by a judge having the force of law.

cross-examination Questions asked of one side's witness by the lawyer for the other side. These questions take place after direct examination.

custodial parent The parent having custody.

custody The right to take care of and make decisions for a child. Custody can be sole, joint, shared, physical, and/or legal, each of which carries different rights and responsibilities.

damages Monetary harm caused by someone else's actions.

defendant The person being sued, sometimes also referred to as the respondent.

depose Lawyers asking questions of a witness under oath in the presence of a court reporter or stenographer.

deposition The process of deposing a witness.

deposition transcript   The typed version of what a witness said in a deposition.

direct examination   Questions asked of one side's witness by that side's lawyer.

disbarment   Taking away a lawyer's license to practice law.

discovery   The process leading up to a trial during which the lawyers obtain information about the other side's case by using depositions, interrogatories, and other means.

dissolution   The process of ending a marriage.

divorce   What is required to legally end a valid marriage.

docket   A list of cases kept by the court.

domestic-relations law   Law having to do with marriage, divorce, child custody, visitation, alimony, child support, and adoption. Sometimes also referred to as matrimonial or family law.

domicile   The place where someone lives.

estate   All the assets owned by someone.

evidence   Things that are used at trial to prove your case— can include testimony of witnesses, photos, films, and documents.

expert witness   A witness who is qualified by education or training to render an opinion at trial. Expert witnesses in divorce and custody cases include financial experts, who place a value on assets, and psychologists or social workers, who render opinions regarding suitability of child-custody arrangements.

family law   *See* domestic-relations law.

father's rights   Legal principles and concepts used to further the notion that custody decisions should not discriminate against fathers.

fee/retainer agreement   The contract between lawyer and client outlining their responsibilities to each other. For maximum clarity, it should be in writing.

grounds   Reasons.

hearing   The process whereby each lawyer tries to orally persuade the judge to do something. A hearing is shorter than a trial and usually addresses only one or two smaller issues.

hearsay   What someone claims he or she was told by someone else. Sometimes hearsay cannot be used as evidence in a trial.

interrogatories   Written questions that must be answered under oath within a certain time period.

judgment   The final court-ordered result of a trial or of a lawsuit.

jurisdiction   A location, such as where suit can be filed, where a court has power, or where certain laws are in effect.

litigate   To fight a legal dispute in court.

litigation   The process of fighting a legal dispute in court.

magistrate   A person who performs the functions of a judge but does not have the power to issue a court order. Judges often delegate work (such as hearings and trials) to magistrates/masters who then make recommendations to the judge.

master   *See* magistrate.

matrimonial law   *See* domestic-relations law.

mediation   A process whereby a neutral person known as a mediator attempts to help disputing parties reach agreement voluntarily.

mediator   A neutral person who runs the mediation process.

motion   A request to the court to issue an order for a certain purpose, such as a motion to extend the time limit for answering interrogatories.

no-fault divorce   A divorce that can be obtained without one spouse having to prove the other spouse was legally at fault.

objection   What a lawyer says when something is happening in a trial or deposition that is inappropriate. This is one of the many steps involved in protecting the record.

opening statement   The lawyer's opening remarks to the judge at the beginning of the trial.

opinion   A belief held by someone. Usually witnesses are limited to stating facts in court and cannot give their opinions unless they are qualified as expert witnesses.

paralegal   A person who assists a lawyer in much the same way that a nurse assists a physician.

parenting classes   Classes that teach parents how to minimize the negative effects of divorce on their children.

petition   To request something from the court; to ask.

plaintiff   The person filing a lawsuit, sometimes also known as petitioner or complainant.

pleadings   Papers filed in court during a lawsuit.

precedent   Something that has already happened that will influence how future similar events will be viewed by the court.

preserving (or protecting) the record   A complex and important series of actions a lawyer must take during a lawsuit to lay the groundwork for an appeal.

proposed findings   Conclusions reached by a master or magistrate that he or she recommends the judge agree with.

putting on a case   Presenting evidence to the judge during the trial.

rebuttal   Evidence the plaintiff can put on after both sides have concluded their cases to respond to points made for the first time during the defendant's case.

recommendations   Actions the master or magistrate thinks the judge should take.

recross   A second round of cross-examination that occurs after redirect.

redirect   A second round of direct examination that occurs after cross-examination.

release   A document that gives up a person's right or claimed right to something. A release is usually given in exchange for something else, typically another release or money.

remand   The act of sending a case back to the trial judge to be tried again because the judge made a significant mistake the first time.

restraining order   A court order stating that a person may not do a certain thing. Restraining orders are sometimes sought by one spouse to try to prevent the other spouse from committing violent acts or stalking the spouse seeking the restraining order.

retainer   The sum of money initially paid to hire the lawyer.

sanctions   Court-ordered punishment.

separation   A husband and wife no longer living together.

settlement   Way of ending a lawsuit by mutual agreement instead of by court decision.

subpoena   Legal document requiring the presence of a person or things at a designated place and time.

surrebuttal   Evidence the defendant can present to counter rebuttal evidence.

testimony   Words spoken by witnesses under oath at a trial or deposition.

transcript   Typed version of testimony and other words spoken at a trial or deposition.

trial   The process whereby both sides orally present legal arguments and evidence to a master, magistrate, or judge.

uncontested divorce   A divorce that the parties agree on.

visitation schedule   A list of dates stating when each parent sees each child.

waiver   Giving up the right to something such as child support, or giving up the right to challenge the fact that an error was made at trial that caused a problem.

witness   A person having knowledge of facts or other information.

Index

Abuse. *See* Domestic violence
and abuse; Sexual abuse
by spouse
Accessibility/responsiveness of
lawyer, determining,
55–57
Acquaintances, getting lawyer
recommendations
from, 28
questionnaire, 145–49
Action plan
firing lawyer for failure to
follow, 128–29
obtaining, 86–91
and prioritizing goals,
109–10
sticking to, 91–93

Actions, 205
Adversarial divorce, 24–25
Advertising by lawyers, 29
Agreements, 205. *See also*
Fee/retainer agreements;
Prenuptial agreements;
Settlement agreements
Allegations, 205
American Academy of
Matrimonial Lawyers, 33
Annulment, 205
Appeals, 16–19, 205
determining lawyer's
familiarity with, 49
Appellant, 205
Appellate court, 205
Archie, Vivian, 124